10 SECRETS MY DOG TAUGHT ME

10 SECRETS MY DOG TAUGHT ME

Life's Lessons
from a
Man's Best Friend

CARLO DE VITO

MJF BOOKS

NEW YORK

Published by MJF Books
Fine Communications
322 Eighth Avenue
New York, NY 10001

10 Secrets My Dog Taught Me
LC Control Number 2008920191
ISBN-13: 978-1-56731-924-8
ISBN-10: 1-56731-924-6

This book is dedicated to my parents,
Who taught me a deep love of all animals, especially dogs.

It is also for my two boys, Dylan and Dawson,
Who, I hope, will also come to understand the invaluable
and incalculable contribution animals make to our lives.

And to my wife, Dominique,
She is a kinder, more compassionate, and more passionate animal lover
and expert than I could ever be.

And of course to my friend Exley,
Who will be with me all the rest of the days of my life.

CONTENTS

Exley
March 7, 1991 — May 13, 2002

"Properly trained, a man can be
dog's best friend."
— *Corey Ford, American writer*

PROLOGUE

As I remember it, it was somewhere around 4:45 in the morning. That's around the time I first heard him whine. I remember the big red digital numbers screaming out at me from the darkness of the nightstand. Exley was awake. He was always an early riser. Even at the ripe old age of 9, when he had finally learned how to relax, as soon as the sun first peaked over the roofline of the house across the street, Exley was awake. What was unique about this particular morning was that the sun was not yet out.

Exley was a stout, athletic German shorthair pointer. His chocolate-brown head and hazel-to-light-brown eyes sat alertly atop his gray-, white-, and brown-flecked body, which was dotted like an exclamation point by his stubby little tail. If you make a fist, but free up the thumb and then wave it back and forth as fast as you can, that's what Exley's tail looked like when he was happy.

Exley was looking out our bedroom window rather intently. He was whining as if there was a squirrel or a stranger standing on the roof of the porch, which sprung out from underneath our bedroom window. But it was winter, and it was very dark. And I shushed him. He persisted. And then I think I tried several more shushes until I threw a slipper or magazine at him. Each time, he would hrumph and then make three circles in his dog bed before finally collapsing, disgruntled. Each time, he let out a big sigh. But several minutes later, he would start pacing the room again and looking out the window and whining. I refused to get up that early in the morning. I knew this wasn't about having to go out. His little tail was going as fast as it could, back and forth, and our white German shepherd, Chelsea, was wound up like a big ball of fur on the floor. Even she was trying to shut him out that early in the morning. I think I threw a magazine across the room at one point. But it was to no avail. My wife gently elbowed me in the ribs, telling me to either make him stop or take him downstairs. Now I had to get up.

I got out of our warm and comfy four-poster bed. As I did, Exley jumped up and down with joy and raced back to the window. I walked across the creaky floors of our 100-year-old Victorian home to pull open the drapes and see what all the fuss was about.

"What the hell is out there?" I asked him. He looked up at me, his face bright and excited, his tail at fan speed. You would think I was about to give him a big cookie or something. I peaked through the curtains, and I understood. The house had been coated with almost a foot of snow. Exley let out an excited bark. And I knew in a moment that I was done in. I knew then that Exley would not relent. There was snow. And Exley loved the snow.

I dressed as fast as I could, but still half asleep, I tripped and fell to the floor while I was trying to pull up my pants. My wife groaned and rolled over. Exley and I made our way downstairs. I put my coat and boots on and opened the door. He shot out of the house like a Thoroughbred at Churchill Downs. He bounded off the deck in one leap to the ground. And as was his habit, he put his head all the way into the snow, walked a few paces as if he was sniffing the ground underneath it all, and then flipped his head up and shook it, and then repeated the actions again and again.

He ran around the yard. I threw snowballs for him to fetch. He would pounce on the landing site like a bear after salmon. He trundled through the heavy snow, his big brown floppy ears flapping up and down against the frosty-white backdrop. We stayed out for what seemed like hours.

This is one of my favorite memories. And it was one of the things I will always carry with me that my dog taught me:

Enjoy the simple things. Cherish them. Exley helped me remember what fun it is to play in the snow. More often than not, the mention of snow at midlife conjures up only the terrifying, backbreaking reality of having to shovel all that stuff up. Dig out the car. Carve a path where the sidewalk used to be.

Exley's lesson on that day was to remind me how really fun snow can be, and to stop and recognize the simple pleasures in life. Whether it was a bone, a walk, or a favorite treat. It didn't have to be that fancy. Maybe for me, despite a love of wines, a favorite moment is with a simple burger and a beer. Maybe yours is a small bit of chocolate, or a nice warm, luxurious bath. Maybe it's just sitting on the sofa on a rainy day and listening to the drops hit the earth.

As time passes, I reflect on moments like these. Some moments I cherish; others are painful. But in each of these events, I find some life lesson. Some I recognized at the time; others I had to think on before their meaning was revealed. But in the end, that dog taught me a lot. He taught me many lessons, lessons I could use elsewhere in life. And I have tried to remember them in my personal life, in my dealings with family members, and in my dealings with friends and business associates. He was a pretty damn good teacher, if you ask me.

INTRODUCTION

"We find rest in those we love, and we
provide a resting place in ourselves
for those who love us."
— *Saint Bernard of Clairvaux*

I have written several dog books, and in them, I have written of Bentley and Exley many times. I did so without thinking. They were both mile markers in my life. And when it came time to dispense any working knowledge of dogs and caring for dogs, I did so by using my life with them (and other dogs we have been lucky enough to know) to illustrate points or techniques.

When I wasn't writing, my wife, Dominique, and I were both horrific "stage mothers." I spent one morning in Brooklyn freezing my toes off in the frozen tundra of Prospect Park, waiting with other owners and dogs to have them filmed on Fox News, where the morning show promised viewers, "dog carolers" during the Christmas season. Exley's nose almost smudged the camera lens at one point. His television experience also included an ill-conceived spot on the short-lived Lifetime morning show *Biggers and Summers* in 1995. He was brought on to do a dog massage segment but was put on stage with a perfectly nice Akita, who nonetheless inspired great excitement in Exley. He also had a distinguished literary career. Aside from being featured in my own books, he appeared in *An Owner's Guide to a Happy Healthy Pet* (by Nancy Campbell) and *On the Trail with Your Canine Companion* (by Cheryl S. Smith).

In life, we were constant companions, Exley and I. We could annoy the hell out of each other, groan, be grumpy, and moan at each other. I laughed off his manic reactions to squirrels, and he ignored my violent ravings at the New York Giants on Sundays in the fall.

We shared a deep love of the woods and of long walks, enjoying fields and forest floors. We both loved beer, and most foods. He never understood my occasional love of cigars, and I never understood his insatiable appetite for garbage cans.

He was as gaseous a dog as ever was born, especially when he got older. He could clear out a whole room in seconds. There were many times, around the dining room table or in the living room or den, when suddenly, and without warning, a great howl would utter forth. Not from the dog, but from the family, screaming in terror at the attack that had been leveled against our retinue.

That said, we were perfect friends. We shared 10 good years together. He was a friend, confidant, buddy, and hellion. And I loved him for it. He had a zest and an excitement for life that did not abandon him until the last breath left his body. And I loved him as much as or more than most of my family. He was one of us.

And of course, the thing about friendship, what many of us do not realize, is that the gifts of the friendship keep giving long after one of you has moved on. The lessons, the laughter, the tears, and the comforts are all remembered.

I guess my fondest memories of Exley have to do with the fall and the woods. The two of us walking around. I could take a dozen dogs through the forest the rest of my life, and I wouldn't ever reach the same sense of simpatico that I reached with him. Sometimes I walk in the woods alone these days. I might stop and walk the old, familiar grounds. I don't tell my wife. I walk, and smile, and warm myself with happy memories about him. Some may think it strange, but those of us who've had dogs who were our friends understand.

I almost burst into laughter and tears simultaneously when

I read this quote from Mary Carolyn Davies: "A good dog never dies, he always stays, he walks besides you on crisp autumn days when frost is on the fields and winter's drawing near, his head is within our hand in his old way."

Exley will always be my puppy and my friend.

1 | YES, THERE IS SUCH A THING AS LOVE AT FIRST SIGHT

"How rare and wonderful is that flash
of a moment when we realize
we have discovered a friend."
—*William E. Rothschild, American writer*

Seeing my dog for the first time and meeting my wife confirmed for me that there is something good in the universe. There are two things I remember very clearly that speak to the subject of this chapter. I remember the first day I saw my wife, and I remember the first day I saw this dog. Done. Was I predisposed to liking either? Probably not. There were plenty of dates I'd gone on where I figured out I didn't like them, and plenty vice-versa as well. But when I finally met Dominique, I knew it was right.

And there have been many subsequent times when my wife and I went to look at dogs for adoption and returned them to their kennel, sad and disappointed but sure we were turning down an animal that wasn't right for us. No, seeing Spike (as he was called then) was indeed, silly as it sounds, love at first sight.

THE SEARCH

I can't help but laugh when I think of the arrogance it must have seemed like when I walked into a colleague's office more than a dozen years ago and asked him for the name of a dependable breeder—and he refused. I was a young editor at Macmillan Publishing Company, on Third Avenue, not too far from the famed P. J. Clark's. In the late 1980s and early 1990s, I was a cocky, aspiring Michael Korda with a couple of decent books to my credit when I walked into the office of one of the executives and announced that I wanted a German shorthair pointer. He was the vice president of Howell Book House, considered at that time the premiere pet publisher in the world.

In short, this VP was appalled. He was easily one of the two or three most influential dog book editors in the entire country. He was a short man with a large forehead and handlebar mustache. He could be as opinionated as any college campus intellectual. But he was also more than willing to swap stories about almost anything, especially Brooklyn, which was where he lived with his wife and half-dozen dogs. He was an accomplished breeder and an American Kennel Club (AKC) judge who had even judged at Westminster. We were both characters in a Dickens novel, and I always found him charming. I explained to him why I thought it was time to own a dog. The idea of me raising a dog, let alone a shorthair, was preposterous to him, and he was more than happy to tell me so.

He practically shouted at me in a shocked manner. "Do you know how much trouble a shorthair will be? You can't clean up your office, let alone care responsibly for a dog. You may want a dog, but I will not commit some poor animal to a life of misery under your direction." If I am not quoting him accurately, I am certainly capturing the sentiment.

His perspective was quite clear to me. It is no understatement to say that I had a less-than-sterling reputation, looking back. I was well known for playing a game of pepper with a bat and baseball in the company corridors with other workers. We used to throw a football down the length of the editorial department, seeing how far we could throw it without touching the walls or ceiling. The ball once skipped into the president's office while he was meeting with his boss from corporate. I was the de facto commissioner of the lunchtime touch football games. And of course, my office was a disaster.

You can guess what these shenanigans might have said

about me to other people. And I suppose if you had asked me point-blank what I was doing these things for, I would have scoffed and said we were just having fun. I don't think I ever gave it much more thought than that. Probe a little deeper, and I suppose I would have told you it made me colorful.

More than one person had told me that I had to "grow up." I often resisted this advice or criticism. I considered my devil-may-care attitude to be one of my more charming qualities. In retrospect, I was probably a bit of a horse's ass.

I knew my colleague was dead serious about the dog. As much as he liked to impress people with his Irish brogue and his racy jokes at office parties, he was no joker when it came to animals. I suppose it was also retribution for all the times I had harassed him about how the judges at the Westminster Dog Show had chosen the wrong dog yet again. Each February, I baited him effortlessly, much to my own and other editors' amusement, because he took me seriously the first few times I baited him. Then one February, when I broached the subject yet again, he just looked up suspiciously and said, "Screw off."

Unfazed, I tried yet another influential editor at Howell. She was a spark plug of a woman who had a laugh almost as loud as mine and whose opinions were just as distinct and un-changeable as her counterpart's. It was company legend that the two fought tooth and nail over the habits of certain breeds or over some dog world personality. If he had an opinion (that's like saying "if a cheetah had spots"), then most certainly she also held as strong an opinion that was exactly opposite.

She laughed when I told her I wanted a dog. But she was slightly more sympathetic. I cannot remember which of the two suggested that I take on a rescue dog. I told them I was flattered that they thought I might take on such an adventurous lifestyle. I envisioned myself and my altruistic companion searching ruins, climbing mountaintops, looking for lost campers, etc. But rescue dogs, I learned, were purebred dogs who had been given up by their owners. Usually they came already house-trained and were slightly older. I scoffed. I wanted a puppy.

I knew something about dogs. I had grown up with dogs. We had owned in some odd order an Irish setter, an English setter, a poodle, and a Dalmatian. My grandfather, an avid outdoorsman, had owned a series of beagles and eventually an English setter named Joe, who as a child I called Jo-Jo. When I was 5, my father was taking care of Jo-Jo after my grandfather died. I opened the door to our enclosed patio so my sister could pet him.

I assured her I could handle him. The excited dog bowled

us both over once the door was opened no more than 3 inches, raced to my parents' bedroom, and proceeded to soil, in every possible way, my mother's white shag carpets.

My mother and stepfather, Anna and Eugenio, owned a Dalmatian named Bentley when I was younger. That dog became my best friend. I knew that a German shorthair pointer would be just as demanding as a Dalmatian. Both are extremely active dogs. Shorthairs were bred to be über-dogs by German sportsmen in the late 1800s. Shorthairs could point, flush, and retrieve game in the open field on 2- or 3-day field trips. Properly trained, they could hunt with you on ground or from horseback. And they took to water with great affection. Shorthairs are great companions for those who like hiking, running, or biking—regularly.

When I was a little boy, and my father, Phil, was in his twenties, he owned a shorthair named Timothy. To a little boy whose parents had just divorced, Timothy seemed like a fun playmate. My father bought a suite of rattan furniture for his new bachelor pad. Upon returning from McDonald's one day, we discovered that Timothy had unwrapped all the furniture. I thought it funny, kind of cool. My father was not similarly impressed. Another time, Timothy ate two cartons of cigarettes. I think that was probably the last straw for Tim. He was gone not long afterward. My father did not have the patience at the time to raise a dog, and he knew it.

I was determined to get a dog and habitually harassed both dog editors until I shook free a name from one of them. I ended up talking with three women: Joan Tabor, Judy Marden, and Nancy Campbell. These three women were the key people in my region as breeders and as volunteers of the GSP Rescue organization. I remember I ended up in a conversation with Nancy Campbell and discussed with her my desire to buy a shorthair. She asked me numerous questions and told me all about shorthairs. As if I didn't know.

Nancy was vigilant about the requirements of a shorthair. As she was more than happy to point out, I was someone who arrived at work no later than 8:30 and left no sooner than 6:00 p.m. My job and my friends were my life. Nancy said, "No."

"Pardon me," I stammered.

"I certainly won't sell you one of my puppies. You are not properly positioned to bring up a puppy. And I'm not even sure I would match you up with a rescue dog either. I think you should rethink this idea about getting a dog." I was aghast. With people like this selling dogs, no wonder people went to pet chain stores to buy their animals. Whatever happened to customer service? Whatever happened to "the customer is always right"? If all breeders are like this, I naively thought at the time, I should go into the dog-breeding business. I'd make a fortune. I was so arrogant.

Of course, Nancy was doing her job. Responsible breeders screen their potential customers. First, they want to make sure the people who buy their dogs are buying dogs that are right for their lifestyle. It's amazing how many people buy animals because they like the way they look and know nothing about the dogs' traits. Second, Nancy didn't want the dog back—or, worse, destroyed in some distant dog pound, abandoned by disillusioned owners.

Of course, I wouldn't listen to Nancy and bombarded her with phone calls until I convinced her of my sincerity to raise the dog properly. As I countered in later conversations, I lived near a large park, Prospect Park, which had a rich and diversified dog population and plenty of room to run. I could offer morning and evening walks that would be great fun for the dog.

"I think I might have one for you. He's a real couch potato, and he's 5, so he's starting to calm down," Nancy told me. But disappointingly, someone else was able to show up before me, and they took him. I was then offered a 10-year-old female. I refused. If I owned another dog, I might have considered caring for an older dog. But I didn't want to take in an older dog as my only pet and develop an attachment so near its end.

My father looked at a couple of big males in New Jersey. He is a big, imposing man. Several people have told me that he reminds them of Anthony Quinn. With his deep brown eyes and large paws for hands, he is fond of dogs. He has often told me stories of his father and his father's many beagles. He knows dogs well, especially hunting dogs. I was very hopeful, especially about one of them.

"A bust. The first one was too big. He was huge. No good," Phil said.

"And the other?"

"He was gorgeous. But he won't work."

"Why?"

"A cat killer."

"Did the owner tell you that?"

"No!" he scoffed. "I could tell. He was a big SOB, and he had that look in his eye. He would take one look at your girlfriend's cat and make it lunch. Not good with kids either." At the time, I was dating rather seriously a publicist who had a cat. I needed a dog who could get along with a cat. And so my search continued. It was starting to seem pointless, and I was considering not buying a shorthair, but maybe switching to a Dalmatian. Then came the call of a lifetime.

"I have one. I wouldn't normally have thought of you for him, but I think you should come up and take a look at him," said Nancy warily. "His name is Spike."

BOY MEETS DOG

Nancy tried to lower my expectations before I went up to her home in Connecticut. Spike was a problem child. He had been sold by a reputable breeder to a hunter who did not mention that the dog was destined for an older woman who didn't really want him. Three months later, she gave the dog to another man. Spike ended up being chained to a stake in the ground by a length of no more than 3 feet. Eventually, he escaped this home and was hit by a car. He was treated and returned to his stake in the ground. He escaped again and became feral. He then picked up Lyme disease. He eventually ended up in the Trenton animal control center, where they contacted the shorthair rescue group.

Joan Tabor and Judy Marden, both top Eastern shorthair breeders and rescue volunteers, took turns nursing Spike back to some semblance of health. They had tracked down his breeder, his former owners, and his vet records, scant as they were. They got him caught up on his shots and started trying to train him. Spike was making a nice recovery. Judy had a soft spot for Spike. A well-published expert, she was also the wife of former AKC president Ken Marden. Judy had spent a lot of time with Spike.

Somewhere along the way, he had been shown a couple of times, with some success. Spike came from great bloodlines and was supposedly a handsome dog. However, he had one serious aversion that would put a halt to show biz dreams—he hated being crated. Crating, which seems somewhat horrible to a great many people, is actually a very natural lifestyle choice for dogs, which reinforces their desire for a den. I have since seen many dogs happily race toward their crates, their dens, when crating has been made a positive experience for the dog. Any accomplished show dog must become accustomed to spending time in a crate because of the great amount of time spent on the road.

Judy and Nancy both tried to break him of this aversion, but were met with little success. Apparently Spike was unchangeable in his feelings toward crates. No matter the number of hours Spike was left in a crate, he would bark for the entire time the door was closed.

"Just when I thought we had him, he started barking all over again," Nancy said. She was ready to give up. The fact that Spike had defeated two tough women like Judy and Nancy certainly gave me pause, though I said nothing to either of them. Nancy was especially not someone to be trifled with. And I didn't want to give her any reason to doubt my intentions.

This dog needed a strong owner, Nancy told me. "I know you. I haven't met you yet, but I know you. You cannot be this dog's friend. I know you want someone to play with, but this dog needs a strong owner. He needs discipline. You need to be in control. You need to be firm. You need to be the leader." At the time, I considered Nancy to be a bit harsh, and I down-played some of her warnings to myself. Yeah, yeah. I just yesed her to death. Anything to get to the dog. Yet, I did like her. Her toughness, her outspoken ways, her critical eye, these were all out of her love for the dogs and a sense of responsibility. I re-spected that. There was something about her I admired. Of course, I had no idea how right she was. I was a lughead. We made arrangements to meet.

Nancy later confided that she and her husband, Mark, had taken Spike on a trip to Maine with her puppy, Jilly. She wanted to see if they had made any progress on his obedience. "I let him off his lead on the beach, and he just took off. I mean, I never saw a dog take off like that, ever. And he took my little Jilly right with him!" she related, still in disbelief. "I did everything. I chased him. I called out. Finally, in a panic, I pretended to fall down and get hurt. He came right back to find me, and luckily, Jilly followed him." Nancy grabbed his leash and didn't let go again.

My sister lived in Connecticut at the time and lent a hand. She picked me and my girlfriend up at the Stamford train station, and our little adventure began. The ride to Nancy's rural Connecticut home was long and winding. She and her husband, Mark, owned a lovely clapboard home set off by many trees and a small, crooked driveway. The whole place oozed that New England Yankee rural charm. We were all completely jealous. It was a partly sunny November day, with dappled light playing off the trees. We got out, and I scanned the house. There were a number of shorthairs racing around the yard. Each one was more beautiful than the other. I thought I had died and gone to heaven.

Nancy came out of the house. She had blonde hair and wore a down jacket, jeans, and boots. She had craggy good looks and stuck out her hand. She was very nice and welcoming. It was good to finally meet her after all the hours that we had spent on the phone. I have no idea what she was thinking when she saw me, but I wanted only one thing—the dog.

"Now, before we meet Spike, I want to say to you again, I do not want you to get down on your knees when you play with him. You need to establish yourself as the alpha male. You need to be in charge. You have to be in charge. He's very strong-willed. I know you want someone to play with, and that's nice. But he cannot see you as an equal. I don't want you getting down on your knees. Understand? You need to be in control."

My sister, Claudia, laughed. "Boy, do you have the wrong guy," she scoffed loudly. Her rosy cheeks grew redder after I shot her a dirty look. She tried to stifle her laughter.

Nancy went to an outbuilding, a series of rooms and kennels where she did her work as head of rescue and as a breeder. She opened the door, and out shot the most beautiful dog I had ever seen.

Spike had a deep chocolate-brown head and gray and brown flecking on the rest of his body, with three large chocolate-brown spots. He had four white paws, which dog experts call socks. And he had light brown eyes. I know I threw a ball to him, but I cannot truly tell you what happened the rest of that day. I was so immediately in love with this dog, I paid little attention to anything else.

My overriding memory is Spike in a playing posture, with his front legs splayed out and his head down, inviting me to throw the ball and play. That was his essence. Spike loved the outdoors. He loved running outside, his huge pink tongue falling out the side of his jowly soft mouth, his eyes bright, and his dark ears flapping up and down in the wind as he raced through it.

Rabindranath Tagore, the great Nobel Prize–winning Indian poet, wrote, "Depth of friendship does not depend on length of acquaintance." In Spike's eyes, I could see a friend. Everything Nancy had said to me went right out of my mind. And I am sure to this day that I saw in his eyes the same kind of excitement that I was feeling.

I cannot help but say that I had missed my Dalmatian, Bentley. My parents had bought him when I was in sixth grade, and he became my instant friend. He slept in my room when I was a boy. His death a few years earlier had left a void in my life that I thought would never be filled. His story is a whole other book. As much as I felt I could never replace Bentley, despite dogs I might own in subsequent years, I could not help but look at Spike and wonder.

Bentley was a strong-willed, hardheaded animal. And he was a runner. He was 1 inch too tall and 2 inches too long to show. He had a head like a pointer and a massive chest. He had numerous black spots, one around his right eye. My grandmother,

Nonna Melina, would say to him in the morning, "Bentley, you smudged your mascara again." He was the best friend a young boy could ever have. In Spike, I couldn't help but see the same kind of spark and body and gait that Bentley had had in his youth. I don't know if I believed in karma or reincarnation, but it seemed as if I had found my boyhood friend all over again.

Nancy took my sister and girlfriend inside to explain a few things to them. I went to pick up a tennis ball to throw to Spike, which was among his favorite games, when I slipped on the mud and fell flat on my back. Spike jumped on top of me and started licking my face and trying to take the ball out of my hands. I could not help but laugh uproariously. This was what I had wanted—what those many hours harassing my colleagues and talking on the phone were all about—a dog to play with. I was laughing because I knew I was going to catch hell, and boy, did I ever. Nancy came running out of the house.

"Get up! Get up! What did I tell you? I told you not to do that! I told you not to get down on the ground with him. He cannot see you as an equal." She went on and on. And of course, she was absolutely right. But I didn't care at that moment. I had found the dog I had dreamed about. I had found my friend; I was sure of it.

SPIKE GOES TO BROOKLYN

I laugh every time I see an old Honda Civic. My sister owned one of these little compact cars. I laugh because I remember returning, with her and my girlfriend up front, and Spike and me in the backseat. Spike had happily jumped in the car with me and licked my face as we made our way from late autumn in New England to the epitome of urban life—New York City.

Somewhere early in the trip, Spike let go some wind. It was awful.

"Whew! He's definitely your dog!" my sister screamed hysterically. The poor dog was as excited and nervous as I was. We drove all the way to Brooklyn with the windows open and the heater on. But I never got cold, and Spike never wavered. However, Spike's habit of airing himself out would go on to become family legend, as he later exhibited his dubious talent at all the right moments, much to our chagrin.

"Each friend represents a world in us, a world possibly not born until they arrive, and it is only by this meeting that a new world is born," Anaïs Nin once wrote. And so it was with this dog.

With an adjustable lead, I happily paraded Spike around the block once we were back in Brooklyn. He sniffed animatedly, marked as much territory as he could, and wagged his stubby little tail. I may have been 29 years old, but I might as well have been 6. My feet weren't even touching the ground. There was not a prouder man in Brooklyn that day.

But we still had much to do. There were two things I wanted to accomplish. One, Spike needed a name change. I hated the name Spike. Just a personal thing. If I had a Doberman, a Rottweiler, or a bull terrier, especially, Spike would have been perfect. But for this dog, it was just the wrong name. And the other thing was to get him to an obedience class as soon as possible.

I came up with a number of names. Several assistants at the time gathered in my office to discuss the various possibilities. I liked the idea of naming him something like Bob or Jerry, or something that would make him sound more human. We thought of some of our literary heroes, i.e. Hemingway, Fitzgerald, Kerouac, and Hunter S. Thompson. None of these seemed right. Finally, I decided on Exley.

Vintage Paperbacks had recently established Vintage Contemporaries, and the line was filled with hip novels that appealed to me and other aspiring New York dilettantes. One of them had caught my eye and instantly became one of my personal favorites, *A Fan's Notes*. Frederick Exley's novel is set in 1950s New York and is about a young man who has replaced the hero worship of his father by becoming fascinated with fellow

USC graduate Frank Gifford. Exley's character follows Gifford to New York and becomes a rabid New York Giants fan.

The novel struck me on several levels. Written in the late 1960s with wit and reverence, Exley recreated the feel of 1950s New York City. It was an eloquent story of a young man spiraling toward a nervous breakdown, and of course, it was about the New York Giants.

If there was anything that in retrospect seems apt, it is the fact that Exley himself was always just slightly out of control. He was a massive smoker and drinker. His binges at the Lion Head Tavern were legendary. As my wife said in anger many years later, "How appropriate you named him after a recalcitrant drunken reprobate!"

Eventually, we just took to calling him Ex. Around Brooklyn, the kids always wanted to pet Exley, thinking he was a Dalmatian.

"What's his name, man?"

"Ex."

"That's his name?"

"Yep."

"Awesome!" Little kids loved to call him Ex. More often than not, when everything at home was cool, we called him Ex. But when we hollered at him, he was Exley.

When it came to training, Exley was uneven. He would heel in the confines of the training center as we wove our way through cones in front of the other participants. One time, after he'd successfully completed a course and earned us great kudos, I turned to congratulate my steadfast companion, only to find him with his leg raised, hosing down one of the cones we had just successfully navigated. But out on the street, Exley would not heel. Getting him to walk with me was a difficult task. I was able to convince him to sit at street corners without much difficulty. Getting Exley to sit, down, and stay was relatively easy. I could make him sit or down without serious threat of him breaking his concentration.

In the house, we had battles royal. Exley liked to sleep on the furniture—any furniture. The sofa, armchairs, and beds were all fair game in his mind. Eventually, we got him to understand that sleeping on the sofa was okay, but not on the bed. Exley and I spent many hours watching television on the couch together. I would hug him while surfing channels, and he'd push his big, double-barreled muzzle into my chest. Exley was a cuddler.

I know it sounds corny to say that there is such a thing as love at first sight, but I also know that there have been times when I have come upon the right thing at home, at work, or with family, and said, "This is right. This is good. It's an automatic." In my job, I have to create books that can compete with thousands of others in the bookstores or in gift shops. Over the years, I've come to call that certain something the "Oooo" factor—that intangible combination of qualities that make a book irresistible. Looking back, there's no doubt in my mind that Exley had the "Oooo" factor. It might not have been love at first sight. But Exley's vigor, playfulness, and vulnerability were the very qualities that appealed to me—whether I was looking for them or not. Add to that the beauty of the German shorthair pointer, and I was done for. I've often thought about the role of the "Oooo" factor as we make our way in the world, and how important it is to everyone.

Whether in my personal life or in my business life, I don't go looking for kismet. You have to just keep searching for the best opportunity. I guess I could have insisted on several other dogs, and I suppose I might have had very nice relationships with some of those animals, but it's not about just getting one; it's about making the connection—and seeing the connection.

I like a lot of my friends' dogs, but that doesn't mean I'd be happier or just as happy with them as I was with Exley.

I guess the idea of love at first sight brands us as optimists. And there's nothing wrong with being a little optimistic. "Love at first sight" doesn't automatically mean that "they lived happily ever after." All relationships have ups and downs.

Whether it's animals, friends, girlfriends, or acquaintances, sometimes you meet someone and you hit it off. It works. Every once in a while in life, everything seems to actually work out. Not often. But when it does, it feels so good. For me, it confirms a sense of something good out there in the world, and that every once in a while, things might actually go my way. When it happens, I thank God, grit my teeth, close my eyes, and hold on for the ride—and I hope it doesn't all fall to hell.

The real goal was to have enough patience to learn the next lesson in my education.

SECRETS TO REMEMBER

- Dogs search for companions just as people do. Finding each other is a joy that will last a lifetime.
- Don't go looking for "love at first sight." It will find you.
- "Love at first sight" doesn't mean you won't have to work hard at it later.

2 DOGS CAN'T OPEN DOORS— AND SOMETIMES NEITHER CAN PEOPLE

"Our real blessings often appear to us in the shape of pains, losses, and disappointments; but let us have patience, and we soon shall see them in their proper figures."
—*Joseph Addison, English essayist and poet*

The one thing Exley and I shared in large part was the same negative trait—neither of us had one lick of patience when we first met. He was as impatient about things as I was. Waiting for anything was difficult for him.

I was impatient with my company for not promoting me faster, quick to judge, and quick to let people know what I thought. I was hard to handle and often went off without a moment's notice. Looking back, in short, I was the kind of employee I would seriously consider discouraging today. I was hard to manage.

Everything took too long. Publishing moved too slowly. Books took too long to make. My career was taking too long to progress. On the personal level, my relationships didn't seem to progress quickly enough to my tastes either. And it seemed the more I pushed and prodded, the more it seemed like my work and relationships struggled. Even with my sense of humor and my ability to laugh at myself, it seemed to me that people and their advice were obstacles to be overcome.

My impatience also extended to my dog. I wanted him to learn his commands, to obey, to be quick to heel, come, sit, down, and stay. It was clear that he was smart. And I expected success. But Exley proved an excellent adversary—and teacher.

WAITING TO GO OUTSIDE

Convincing Exley that it was not in his best interests to urinate in the house was difficult. Since I adopted him in the winter, taking him out for a walk was not always so easy. He had just come from a place where opening the door meant he was immediately outside. At the time, I was living in Brooklyn, near Prospect Park, with my girlfriend, and we had a wonderful brownstone apartment: an entire floor, with a working fireplace. Opening the door to our apartment only let us out into the hallway, complete with a large, elegant banister and staircase that led downstairs to a beautiful pair of double beveled-glass doors, with large brass doorknobs. Exley wasn't able to appreciate the finer details, especially when it meant a delay in getting outside.

The second or third time I opened our apartment door, he peed right in the hallway. I hollered, and so he began to move — still letting out a steady yellow stream. He raced down the stairs, and a zigzag line wound its way down behind him. By the time we got to the front door, he was finished. This zigzag peeing pattern was something Exley would do the rest of his life. Sometimes Exley was so impatient to get going when he got outside, he would try to walk and urinate at the same time, leaving this bizarre pattern in his wake.

During one particularly fierce blizzard, it took me a little too long to get ready as Exley stood by the front door whining. I looked like one of the Three Stooges, trying to dress in my arctic gear: the double sweaters, the hat, the scarf, the gloves, the double socks. Exley looked up at me.

"Wait," I said. "Wait."

He stared me right in the eye.

"Wait," I said.

He continued to look into my eye. He began to whine.

"It'll just be another minute," I said, struggling.

He stopped whining, and I thought I would just make it. Then he looked at me, his face changed, and I knew it, I just knew it. He stared me straight in the eye and lifted his leg. Right there in the hallway of our apartment, right on the door to the hallway outside.

"No! Exley, no!" I screamed, half-dressed and practically falling down, as he stared at me defiantly. I almost fell trying to reach for him. He didn't even flinch as I stumbled. He just let go the stream of relief. In retrospect, the transition from country to city must have been a rough one for Exley. And he was with a man who could barely dress himself. As I cleaned up Exley's accident in full arctic regalia, I wondered what I had gotten myself into.

SWIMMING THE MIANUS

Having Exley gave me immense satisfaction. As a young man in my mid- to late twenties, I was never so proud as I was of that dog. He was in essence my firstborn, and I could not wait to show him off to family and friends. In the weeks following his arrival in Brooklyn, I made trips to New Jersey to visit my father, Philip, and his wife, Joanne, and then to Connecticut to show him off to my mother, Anna, and my stepfather, Eugenio, and my brother and sister.

My mother and stepfather used to have a Colonial white clapboard house on the banks of the Mianus River in Connecticut. The narrow river lolled past beautiful houses dotted with green lawns, gray docks, white Adirondack chairs, and small colorful boats. My parents' house had a huge lawn that rolled down to the water. Looking across the river, you could see boats at anchor, with their empty, rickety lobster pots stacked like building blocks thrown in a pile, bobbing up and down on the shining water. On the most memorable days, the sky was blue, the grass bright green, and the whites crisp and clean—a picture postcard.

It was on such a day that Exley decided he would go for a swim. He was young and precocious. He romped around, tough and strong, still exhibiting the youthful energy and excitement of a puppy.

Though not exceptionally big, Exley had a broad chest and alert, hazel eyes. He could be a terror one minute and an absolute sweetheart the next. A hunting machine, he liked nothing better than to fall asleep with his head on my lap. He was affectionate to a fault. But his penchant for chasing squirrels, birds, cats, and other animals never ended well—especially for him.

Exley loved my parents' backyard and was fond of rooting around in the shore's black, fine, oozy mud. While my mother loved Exley, she was never very happy to see him arrive at her house, for some mischief, despite my protestations, was always imminent. And this particular day was no different.

Exley and I had been working on his training. I decided that the quiet of my parents' unfenced backyard would be a good place to reinforce my position as the alpha male in our limited pack of two. In retrospect, I'm not sure the idea wasn't to show off in front of my parents, proving to them that I was a responsible adult with a handsome, well-behaved dog. I don't think they were watching, but I cut a very dashing figure just in case they did.

"Siiiit," I said quietly, stepping back slowly. "Sit." I used an even, forceful tone. And surprisingly enough, it was working. I was about 25 paces away. I stopped and commanded evenly again, "Down, Exley. Down." He got down and stayed down, and I began moving a little farther and a little farther back. I was the master; I was the alpha male; I was in control. Finally, I was 50 to 60 paces away on our second attempt at the exercise when I broke my own rule, and I said, "Good boy, Exley! Good boy." I said this at the end, because no matter how I said it, quietly, excitedly, evenly, Exley would break. If anything else, he was consistent in this. No matter the tone, he always broke when I praised him.

In our early training, Exley had always been good at coming back to me. And here he was, running toward me. His ears flopped up and down, his big pink tongue swung like a rag doll from his mouth. A puppyish prance in his step, he bounced toward me. But suddenly, his eyes narrowed, his ears pricked up, his tongue drew in, and his mouth closed. His gait changed from a bouncy trot to a thundering gallop. His powerful chest tightened, and his stride exploded. He raced down the slope of my parents' lawn like a horse in the Light Brigade. I tried to step into his way, but he barely lost stride, changing directions with speed and accuracy not seen since the Roman cavalry. I did not seem to exist.

The ground shook as he approached and then shot past me. Even as I was hollering, "Exley, come here!" at the top of my lungs, I could not help but admire his magnificent elegance while in a full burst of pure speed. His body bobbed like an engine piston, with the grace of a Thoroughbred, but his head stayed fixed like a cheetah in midhunt.

And then he leapt. I can still remember yelling "Nooooo" in slow motion, like in a bad movie. His leap was magnificent. In midair, he was the image of natural beauty. He rose high over the shimmering water, his front paws elegantly stretched out before him, his hind legs balancing his back, and his Goofy-like ears flapping in the wind. And into the beautiful New England postcard Exley leapt. His splash shattered my mental postcard into 1,000 pieces.

"Exley, come! Exley, come here now! Exley!!!" But there was no penetrating his thick head. I scanned the water. There were three boats in the vicinity. But where was he going? There were no birds. I had seen him swim after ducks and seagulls. He was obsessed with game of any kind. I called and called, but he did not heed me. He paddled furiously. One boat missed him. Another boat passed and obscured my view. None of these distracted him. Then it occurred to me. He was swimming to the opposite shore!

"No! No! Come back!" I screamed, but Exley kept moving. Peering between the boats and houses and other obstacles, I tried to see what was drawing his attention. But I couldn't see a thing. Then I realized that I needed to move quickly. I raced up the lawn, ran into the house, swiped the keys, and raced to the car. I had to get to the other side. If my parents were watching, they were probably a little impressed, but not surprised.

I roared down the sun-dappled, crooked country road, honking at anyone in my way. Getting across the river was no easy feat. I had to race up toward Route One, drive across, and find the road on the opposite bank. It should have been easy, but Murphy's Law was like gravity at 10-plus that day. Finally, I raced down the road, opposite my mother's house, finding the landmarks I had picked out before I left.

Once there, I frantically searched the riverbank. I looked at houses Exley might have been tempted to investigate. I checked out a couple of garbage bins that might have offered a tasty reward. I began to worry that he might have been killed by an oncoming car. I drove up and down the street, making sure he wasn't crumpled on the side of the road. What had I done?! Oh, how could I have let something happen to him? It was then that I noticed that near the opposite shore, people on a passing boat were pointing to something. It was Exley crawling back onto land—onto my parents' lawn. He was emerging from the tidal waters, covered in mud, rising like some canine version of the Creature from the Black Lagoon. He shook himself off, his large ears flapping and his stubby little tail wagging away. I was never so happy in my life. He was safe!

Just as suddenly as he had bolted past me into the water, I saw him bolting toward my parents' house. I could see from this distance that the patio door was open. He bounded faster and faster, coated in earthy slime, up the trim cut lawn, toward the striped-awning covered patio and my parents' house. "Noooooooo!" I cried in anguish as he disappeared into the house.

Exley was banished from my parents' house that day. The mud had been tracked throughout. My mother screamed at him. My father screamed at him. I screamed at him. I yanked him outside to give him a bath, and when I was sure my parents weren't anywhere near, I got on the ground and hugged him as never before. And I laughed; I laughed so heartily. I laughed because I loved him and was so happy he was okay. He licked my face and wagged his stubby little tail. He smelled awful, simply awful, and I hugged him all the more.

PATIENCE

Patience is one of those great qualities in a human being that I do not possess in sufficient quantity. Developing patience is something I had to learn in training my dog, and it has helped me in my other relationships.

I look back now, and I can only realize with a little bit of pondering that in many more ways than I would like to admit, I was very much like Exley. I was impatient, especially when it came to other people and their perceptions of me. And I was very impetuous, always racing off, instead of considering the values of my actions.

This was true both in my personal life and in my professional life. In my personal life, like Exley, I sometimes charged head-on, not really thinking where it was I was going, jumping off into some breach I hadn't truly considered. I could be preoccupied with the New York Giants, a recent literary novel, or a wonderful new hobby. I could be romantic one day and completely preoccupied with something else the next. Working with Exley in this period taught me something about patience.

For as difficult as Exley sometimes was to teach (and he could be obstinate), I never tired of trying. Oh, I may have given up occasionally, but I always found myself trying again and again. And as much as I felt frustrated by my inability to get across the lessons to Exley, I never tired. And I realize now, I didn't mind. The reward of finally teaching a command, or getting him to understand a concept, was so rewarding, so fulfilling, that all the hard work getting there paled in comparison. I didn't realize it then, but I was learning something like patience.

I sometimes think I was slightly more mature as a child, suffering through my parents' divorce, than when I was in my early twenties. My father, Philip, once told me, "You're a late bloomer, kid. Don't worry about it." I was really hurt. But he was right. As I look back, I was a late bloomer. I sometimes think I might have achieved a lot more earlier in life if I had had more patience and focused a little more.

I look back sometimes, and I think, "Was I as patient with Exley as he was with me?" Here I was, so proud of my work with Exley. In my lifetime, my parents had owned many dogs, but few were as well trained as Exley. He could sit, stay, and down. When I called him, he came. I worked hard and over many years to make it happen. It did not happen as I had planned. It took a long time for me to understand the many tips and tricks it takes to teach a dog. We were both learning, but in the end, we understood each other.

Exley and I learned to be patient with each other. He ignored my foolishness and outbursts, and I turned my cheek at some of his. But in the end, we both learned a certain amount of discipline. Then, I thought words like *discipline* and *patience* were awful, weighty words. It slowly dawned on me that they were not. In my business and personal affairs, I sometimes lacked discipline and self-control. I expressed my sense of frustration at each turn, but I persevered anyway. Like with Exley, each little step forward helped me to better deal with each setback. I look back now and realize my education was as painful and slow as Exley's. But slowly, we were both beginning to get it.

I first saw this lesson begin its magic on me at work, where I developed much more patience and much more discipline putting proposals together. I dotted I's and crossed T's and took my time preparing the paperwork so I wouldn't look so roughshod when I made my presentations. And it began to pay off.

I also realized that sometimes criticism could be construc-
tive—not just a roadblock. I tried listening a lot harder to others, to see if I could counter or incorporate others' suggestions into my proposals.

When I think back on it now, "there but for the grace of God," if you know what I mean. It wasn't just my learning about patience with Exley, but I think back and wonder, maybe as Exley might have at one point, why did people in my personal and professional lives suffer all of my idiocy?

I am not sure what Exley saw in me. He tried so hard to do what was asked of him, and sometimes I didn't know the right way to ask. And that was probably true with many of my relationships, both personal and professional. Sometimes we are patient with some and not with others. Sometimes it is others being patient with us.

- Patience is one of the most necessary and most difficult self-disciplines to master.

- Developing patience when you are dealing with a dog who does not understand is essential.

- No great achievement was ever accomplished through the virtue of impatience.

- Dogs, children, spouses, and workers require your patience most and are those who get it least. We need to understand them better and make sure we are explaining ourselves as best we can.

- Sometimes, we are impatient with others when we are really most impatient with ourselves.

- Sometimes, it's really about others having patience with us.

3 GOING FOR A WALK IS A GOOD THING

> "Some people see more in a walk around the block than others see in a trip around the world."
>
> —*Anonymous*

There are different kinds of walks. Some walks are taken alone. Around the block. Maybe you walk in a park of some kind. My favorite walks took place in the woods with Exley. But we had all kinds of walks. Sometimes, it was just a walk, but sometimes, it could be so much more. There were several that held special meaning and still resonate when I think about my life with Exley.

As a young adult finding my way in the world, the concept of responsibility was not something I can say I mastered. I was inconsistent and sometimes lazy and prone to cut corners or to find the fast out. As a shorthair, Exley needed lots of exercise. There was no way to cheat or cut corners on this. There was no quick fix. He needed to be walked every day. He needed a long, good walk. A quick once around the block was not going to cut it.

It became obvious quickly that if I didn't walk him, he would get kind of punchy, pace the apartment, and whine a lot—be restless. If I walked him, gave him a good stretch of the legs, say 30 to 40 minutes, he would come home sated and relax, sleeping away the rest of the day.

As Exley and I settled into our lives together, I was compelled to think about the objections my colleagues had to my getting a dog and pondered if maybe they had been right. I started to see a little more seriously what the consequences of my lifestyle might be. It took Exley's arrival and my great love for him to force me to begin to change in ways I had never before thought about. Even things as inconsequential as a walk were beginning to change me in ways I hadn't expected.

This was going to be tougher than I thought.

SOMETIMES A FRIEND IN THE PARK IS A GOOD THING

Prospect Park is one of the most beautiful parks in the world. It was designed by Frederick Law Olmsted, the architect of Central Park. Many Brooklynites think it is superior to Central Park. It is filled with small venues, beautiful streams, and a lake. The park is dotted with old-fashioned street lamps and beautiful brick walkways, and there is a gorgeous boathouse that looks like a beautiful Palladian-windowed wedding cake.

There's also an old-fashioned carousel, and of course, the spectacular entrance at Grand Army Plaza with the Arch of the Grand Army of the Republic (which celebrates the heroes of the Civil War). One cannot help but be reminded of a time in Brooklyn's history when Park Slope was its second-richest neighborhood, studded with gorgeous, elegant brownstones, lined with slate sidewalks and thick, large, leafy trees, and dotted with multigabled churches of various denominations. This is the Brooklyn few outsiders know.

The park is peopled with runners and lots of young families of all shapes, sizes, and ethnicities. It is a place of community. What I also liked about it was that the leash laws at the time stated you could have your dog off-lead from 6 a.m. to 10 a.m. Being able to forgo the leash in New York City was a real plus, no matter the time of day.

This was Exley's most favorite time — the visit to the park. Today, however, was a special day. Exley had sliced his paw on a shard of glass several weeks earlier, and we had not been to the park since.

While he was convalescing, he had been bad about licking his injured foot, which of course, made it worse. At one point, we needed to place an Elizabethan collar on him. If you haven't had to do it yourself, then you've probably seen the large inverted traffic cones that injured or recuperating dogs sometimes sport. He found it most uncomfortable. While it stopped him from licking his foot, Exley became the most dangerous injured dog ever to walk the earth. He could not walk or trot anywhere in the house without the large plastic cone bumping into something. I would be in another room and hear a loud thud as the collar caught on a piece of furniture or a doorjamb. Whereas he could once easily glide underneath the dining room table, he was now completely blockaded and frustrated. At night, he might get out of bed, followed by a series of knocks, pings, thuds, and occasional crashes.

As the days progressed, Exley paced more and more often. And the more he paced, the more stuff he broke. He spent time in front of the window, looking outside, watching the squirrels climb the trees. As each furry tail scampered across the tree limbs, Exley howled and barked and then paced some more. By the time Saturday morning came, I could not get up soon enough to take him to the park and let him run off his steam. And I was excited—to see my friends.

That morning, he tugged on our short walk into the park like an animal clawing at the earth, as if he might slip off, pulling on the lead, aware that we were finally going back to the park. Exley desperately wanted to run in the park, play with the other dogs, and hunt squirrels. For 2 weeks, he'd been under house arrest, and now he was getting out. He was jumping up and down and practically crying.

When we finally crossed the inner roadway of the park and breached the gateway to the great lawn that stretches from one end of Prospect Park to another, Exley howled, still straining at the leash. He was pulling and pawing so much that I had difficulty letting him off the leash, but eventually I managed. I also managed to cut my finger as the catch finally gave.

Exley was off like a rocket. He thundered down the slope of the large green expanse, his giant brown ears flopping. He raced past the small crowd of owners, who had assembled in the early mist of a beautiful Saturday morning in October. His friends, a small pack of Dobermans, were already chasing balls and playing tug-of-war. But I noticed something as Exley neared the usual Prospect Park gang. He wasn't slowing down as he neared them. His pace was as fast as ever. I couldn't believe my eyes as he just plowed straight into another dog. He hit the dog with his chest, his head held high, about midsection.

As one might imagine, the Doberman was knocked down, as was Exley. They both got up snarling. There was much gnashing of teeth and a few snaps, but no blood was drawn, thankfully.

Exley then went into his play posture and spread his front paws out as wide as he could. He lowered his head with an animated look on his face. He barked a few times, and the pack of dogs were now all looking at him. He barked some more. He then spun around, chasing his tail three or four spins in a row, and shot out and ran around the owners and dogs as fast as he could two or three more times. He barked the entire time. The other dogs stared at him, curious, but unimpressed.

Exley returned to his play posture, with no one accepting his entreaty. He harassed each one of his usual friends in the same manner. My fellow dog walkers and I all looked at each other and laughed. Cabin fever still had its grip on Exley, and I think I made the right decision after discussing it with them, that Exley and I would go off through the woods for a little bit and see if he couldn't let off a little steam.

One of the joys of bringing Exley to Brooklyn was the new community of dog owners in the park. As advertised, New York can be a pretty rough place to get to know your neighbors, so the dog run became an important part of my (and

Exley's) social life. It was not uncommon to run into another dog person on Seventh Avenue, in Park Slope, and say "Oh, you're Rohan's mom" or "Hey, aren't you Kiah's dad?" much in the same way parents eventually meet the parents of their children's friends. Two weeks of missing early-morning chitchat—what stores were opening, what restaurants were closing, what movies each of us had seen—I was disappointed to have to move on so quickly.

Exley ignored my new direction at first, but eventually followed because none of his usual partners in crime were willing to play. I took some of the winding paths through the woods for about half an hour. Exley first raced through the woods, and I couldn't help but admire how his body seemed to be performing exactly what it was created for. He darted this way and that through the fallen leaves, moving swiftly and gracefully between trees and over fallen branches, sidestepping a boulder or great rock here and there. Eventually, he got down to the business of hunting, and his nose began brushing the forest floor, looking for clues—usually for squirrels or any other live game.

We went out to the lake, and I threw a big stick into the water again and again. Exley barked and barked and barked, until I threw the wet stick again, his little tail flashing back and forth. When I threw it, Exley bounded for the water and entered with a belly flop. He loved it. While Exley and I were playing at the water's edge, we ran into other friends of ours.

My friend and his dog, a mutt with mostly husky characteristics, joined us. The dogs chased sticks in the pond while my friend and I caught up with each other. We talked sports and movies. We complained about our jobs, talked about our girlfriends, and discussed plans for the weekend. This seemed to go well. My friend was ready to go back, and I decided it might be time to go back out to the lawn.

This time, when I reentered the lawn from the woods, Exley trotted out onto the field, alert and upbeat, but calmer than his first rash appearance. His bouncy gait returned, and he eagerly joined the race for the ball after my friend Kristina threw it. I was finally able to join the usual cast of characters. I told everyone about Exley's recovery as a Conehead, my travails at work, and how much he had missed his friends. We traded gossip and jokes. I could not be happier. The late-October weather was upon us. The dogs were playing, and I was with my friends. I hadn't seen them in weeks, and now I was content.

After some time spent chasing the ball, Exley finally settled into a 20-minute tug-of-war with a large silver Doberman—

one of his favorite playmates and one of his favorite games. When eventually he was lying on the ground, trying to entice other dogs to wrestle him, I knew I had at last tired him out. My friends and I agreed it was time to start our respective days, and I entreated Exley to come for his leash. It was time to go home. He happily complied. We walked back home without incident. Sated.

When we got back, Exley and I both ate breakfast and then relaxed for a while. It was good to see friends. Exley took his leave and sprawled out across the floor and quickly fell asleep.

DARNING HIS SOCKS

Walking in the woods was one thing Exley and I most liked to do together. First, there was our love of nature. Exley's nose scrubbed the forest floor, searching for game to chase (and in his hopes) catch. I can still see Exley's large white paws padding around the fallen leaves.

While there was never truly a bad time to be out with Exley, sunny fall mornings were my favorite. We were usually out there just before or just after sunrise. Exley was an early riser, and he did not take "No" for an answer. Rainy mornings were my least favorite, but walking with Exley in the snow was a lot of fun. I can remember one snowy morning when he had been playing with his dog friends in the park so hard and so steadily that steam rose off his body as he shook off the wet snow.

But no matter the weather, a walk in the woods was, in the end, always a refreshing thing.

As I threw myself into work, it was easy to get lost in the hustle-bustle of urban life. Racing from the subway to the office, to the taxi, to a meeting in another office, was a typical morning. So being "forced" to take time out with Exley in the mornings was a godsend. It provided me with a wonderful window on nature. And there were few walks on which I did not notice some new thing. It was incredible to see nature reveal itself, slowly, as the year ground on. Noticing the buds on the trees starting to swell with life or watching the light green tender shoots and leaves mature into hardy, healthy plants and leaves in the full of summer, watching the slow hand of fall light the trees with the colors of the season, or seeing a beautiful frost coat the forest with its hoary white finger—these were the small wonders, the small miracles, that I would have otherwise missed.

And watching Exley's interaction with his environment was an added joy. I felt like Exley kept me connected with something natural in myself, something too easily lost in the city.

There was a Saturday morning in late spring one year when

we were still living in Brooklyn. It was early in the morning, I remember, because I had to get to work at the Harris Poll. Saturdays and Sundays were our biggest polling days. It was a beautiful day—the sun was up, and it was warm, but not hot. The sky was blue, and the trees were still bright green, the dark green of the long, hot summer not yet baked into their leaves.

In the center of Prospect Park, there's an Adirondack-style gazebo that sits on a point that juts out into a large pond. I sat there with another friend, tossing a stick into the water for Exley to retrieve. Exley chased it with a massive splash and catch, eagerly ready to repeat the feat over and over, as we did. We were on our way back from this idyllic setting when something caught Exley's attention in the brush. I thought nothing of it. This was nothing new, because Exley loved rushing into the brush on our walks. With all the open fields of Prospect Park, Exley learned to sniff the tree line around the park's open spaces, hoping to catch an animal that had inadvertently left the cover of the woods or to roust it from its hiding place.

He whined once inside the brush. He barked once. It was a playful bark, by the sound of it. He whined again, like he did when he was drooling over a dog biscuit or a fresh rawhide bone. I couldn't see him. The cover was deep, with brush and thickets, but I could track him by seeing the tall bushes wiggle. I could hear him easily, though he was 20 feet deep into the brush.

"Come on, Exley. This way! Come on, this way!" I called. I began walking on, which usually got him to forget whatever was distracting him and follow. Then I heard him whine and then let out one bark again. The bushes shook, and then Exley let out a yelp.

"Exley! Exley! Come!" I said angrily. I couldn't reach him. There was no movement. I hollered again, more at him, rather than a call. But now I was concerned. Slowly, he came out of the woods. I saw his head emerge, and he seemed to be walking gingerly, but fine. And then I saw this red thing on his leg. And I remember saying, "What is that you have wrapped around your leg?" When I moved closer, I nearly went into shock.

Exley's right front leg had been ripped open. The skin was down around his foot like a big bloody brown sock. His leg looked like a leg of lamb or pork hanging in a shop window. It looked like meat on the hoof, with veins and muscles and fat. He wasn't crying or whining or whimpering. He sort of just looked up at me, as if to say, "What do we do now?"

He now started a very noticeable limp. I didn't know what

do. There had to be a mile of winding, hilly, tree-lined paths even before we reached the outer ring of the park itself. After a few feet, it became obvious he would not be able to walk the whole way.

It was then that I picked him up and started to jog in an effort to exit the park. I walked and jogged, walked and jogged. I carried him like a shepherd carries a lamb. He hated it. A couple of times I had to set him down. I was panicked. What had happened to my dog? Would they be able to save him?

He felt like a giant sack of flour. He was heavy in my arms, but I found the strength. Somewhere along the way, a friend saw us and told me about a veterinarian who was just outside one of the park entrances. It was early in the morning, around 8:30 or so, but they were open. I ran there, still carrying Exley. I was talking 20 miles an hour. The doctor was slow and methodical. Amazingly, Exley still was not yelping or barking or whimpering. He just stood there, looking around. He hated doctors' offices.

While I was out of breath and scared to death of possibly losing my dog, the doctor seemed most composed and moved slowly and purposefully.

"Will he live?" I asked, feeling stupid but concerned.

"Him?" he said, as if he had forgotten I was in the room.

"Oh, him? He'll be fine. He only desocked himself. He did a good job of it too, but we'll clean it and stitch him back up like brand-new."

"Can I pick him up tonight?"

"No, no, he'll need to spend the night," the doctor clucked. He started working on Exley. I said good-bye to my friend and then I walked out. I gave the nurse my information and left, bewildered. I must have called the doctor's office three or four times that day.

My Saturday and Sunday mornings were ruined. I fretted about my dog constantly. I tried to be macho about it in front of my friends, but inside I was tortured and conflicted. Was I a bad owner and friend for not staying with him? I hoped he wasn't freaked by spending the night at the vet's. Eventually, I picked him up on Sunday, and he was fine. The doctor had done a wonderful job. When I saw Exley, his little tail started wagging, and he gave me big kisses when I knelt down to hug him.

That incident sealed the deal between us. He was not just my friend, as my friends and I joked later; he was my first son. Granted, I was no Dustin Hoffman in *Kramer vs. Kramer*. But just like a parent with a hurt child, I did learn with Exley that at any moment, the unexpected could arise. And was I ever lucky to find that vet on the edge of the park, because I don't know if I could have carried him much farther. But once I got Exley home, I was happy that I had handled the situation as well as I had. I couldn't say that Exley understood what had happened, but there was no doubting that our bond had deepened. We learned a lot about each other on our long walk that day.

ANSWERING THE CALL OF THE JINGLING LEASH

Sometimes, the hardest thing is to answer the bell. There are few dogs who are not excited upon hearing their lead jingle and who don't bound toward the door with great enthusiasm, with the chance of going for a walk.

Unfortunately, especially when I later moved to the suburbs, I found it increasingly easy to stop walking Exley. It's so convenient for homeowners to open the back door, let their dogs do their business in the backyard, and settle back into the couch, watching some football game, a movie, or a television show.

Getting my butt off the couch and making the commitment is what it is all about. A walk is a huge thing in the world of dogs. It's one of the best things you can do if you are truly your dog's friend. Good weather or bad, tired or active, I tried to make a habit of it. There are 1,000 bad excuses (and I have used them all), but there is only one good answer. Of all the things I miss these days, I miss that time I used to take with my friend.

Balance is an important thing. It was important to go on walks alone, and it was also good to make sure we interacted when we went outside. We needed a little of each in our lives. We needed to reach out and see our friends and neighbors, and we also needed time alone so we could reflect on nature, ourselves, and others.

I try to remember that in this world, which seems to spin faster and faster and clang louder and louder every year, I sometimes need to take a step back and appreciate the slow and silent marvels of nature and use these moments to reflect. It sounds so new age, but in fact, it's the secret about nature that most outdoorsmen and -women already know.

In the movie *The Last Picture Show,* Sam the Lion admits that he's been coming to the same body of water for years, yet he knows there are no fish there. "That's probably why I like it so much," he says. Sometimes, it's about the sporting experience, but good day or bad, it's really just about being out there.

It was also important to remember the value of responsibility, commitment, and routine. This was one of the hardest lessons to learn, and one I realized much later. I never thought to myself, "This is my responsibility. This is my job." I took his welfare upon myself like a parent: to make sure my charge was well fed and well taken care of. My only thoughts were of his safety and well-being, of hopefully doing the right thing.

SECRETS TO REMEMBER

- Dogs and people are social beings. Dogs and people depend on social interaction for a sense of self and for validation from their peers.

- Socializing is good for you, because it keeps your communication skills sharp and helps you better deal with people, whether you are at work, at home, or with friends.

- Sometimes a walk alone around the block or out in the woods is a chance to breathe, to clear your mind.

- Making a commitment to go for a walk is very important. Sometimes showing up is half the battle.

- Make a point of looking around when you walk your dog. Don't just walk head-down. Look, smell, hear, and see what is going on in your environment.

- It's a great way to spend time with your dog.

4 OBEDIENCE IS A GOOD THING

"I have thought about it a great deal, and the more I think, the more certain I am that obedience is the gateway through which knowledge, yes, and love, too, enter the mind of the child."

—*Annie Sullivan, American educator,*
teacher of Helen Keller

Kristina Johnsen, a member of my dog clique in Prospect Park, once said to me, "When I first met you, I thought your dog's name was Exley-goddamn-it!" We both had a good chuckle. When I first got Exley, I bought one of those retractable leads. I knew only a few dog people at the time, and many of the walks Exley and I went on were comprised of just the two of us. I used this time to call him and give him a treat when he came back to me. It was a long and arduous process of weeks and weeks of chastisement and reward.

Exley was not quite as obedient as I would have liked, so I rarely let him off the leash. Frankly, I was afraid if I let him off-lead, I would simply never see him again. As Exley and I settled into a groove, I didn't need to be racing across rivers or worrying about traffic every day. One night, I had to go out of town on business, and my girlfriend had to walk the dog. When I returned, I asked her if she had had any problem, and she said no, except for getting him to come back when it was time to go. She'd had to chase him down. She had just assumed that like other owners at the park, I released him once we were inside the park. I was thrilled to know he eventually returned, but I was still somewhat leery of letting him off-leash myself.

The joke was that knowing that he *might* return, I soon started experimenting with letting Exley off-lead. And when he decided to rush off in one direction or another, I would call him, hoping to redirect his newfound energy. With his dark, chocolate-brown head scouring the ground for scents, his little tail fanning back and forth, I knew I was in trouble. When I wanted to turn around or go in another direction, especially in the beginning, I might have trouble with him. I called and called and called, and he ignored me. Eventually I would say, "Exley, goddamn it!" This didn't work either, and I was forced to chase him down.

I don't suggest this method, actually. It's not very effective, it's embarrassing in front of other dog people, and it won't get you in with God or your clergyman. Eventually, I bought an inexpensive 15-foot lightweight cloth leash. I brought Exley to the park and released him with the lead still attached. Like other young dogs, Exley thought returning when I called him was a game. When I called him, he'd come close but then veer off at the last second, the lead dangling behind him. Happily, the training lead provided the brakes I needed. Whenever Exley decided he was going to do a flyby instead of actually returning to me, I stepped on the lead and brought him to a halt. I then repeated the command as I slowly pulled him toward me. Upon his arrival, I would give him a treat.

This was not a fun thing to do, but it was a good next step. I was able to give him the freedom he wanted but the control I needed. Of course, it seemed like he was oblivious to this stage, but he did enjoy the freedom. He dragged that lead through mud, puddles, and countless other unmentionables. It was not always a very exciting leash to pick up. But the hard work was worth it. Eventually, he became more responsive, by degrees, and eventually started working without a training lead. After several months, we reached a point where we could go without.

It was then that I learned how important obedience was.

I've never been a good one for following instructions,

whether they came from a parent or teacher or in a box with a new DVD player. This makes life more difficult than it needs to be. It's the same for dogs. Dogs need to learn a certain amount of obedience, or many people will give them up. The same goes for human beings.

Like other owners, I wanted to give Exley the opportunity to roam and have fun with the hundreds of dogs he so desperately wanted to play with. But inevitably, I was always forced to yell, exasperated, "Exley, goddamn it!" I would be at one end of the park's open, spacious green, and Exley would follow some other dog home, or go chasing a squirrel, or go charging off into the bushes. I called, and there was no recognition on Exley's part. Heedless, he followed his furrowed brow in whatever direction it was pointed. And then I would have to excuse myself from the group of owners, muttering, "Exley, goddamn it!" and go chasing after him. This may seem funny here and now, but I can assure you, as you probably already know, it was definitely not fun at the time.

Over the course of the next several months, I began working with Exley to improve his obedience. I made him work the "down" command right there in the park. And then a long stay. We worked on our commands—especially the command to "come here." This was work that paid off.

Eventually, I trusted Exley. When I let him off-lead, I called him and told him to "come here," and he came back. I was happy and so was he. As he got better at heeding the command, I got more comfortable with him being off-lead. If he was going to listen while being off-lead, then he could stay off-lead longer. And eventually what started happening was that I would let him go a little longer and a little farther away.

After we moved away to the suburbs and bade our many friends in Brooklyn farewell, we discovered bigger parks. Here, Exley could truly roam. Whereas 100 yards seemed my limit in Brooklyn, Exley was free to roam 200 to 300 yards in a park, again, where leash laws allowed for off-lead walks early in the morning hours.

It came to the point where I could almost walk him without a lead (where laws allowed such things). We went to the beaches and other wilderness areas around the East Coast. While he usually found ways to get into trouble, for Exley was rarely far from trouble, he seldom failed to return when called.

It was at this point in our relationship, after 2½ to 3 years to-gether, that both Exley and I learned something. The more he obeyed, the more freedom he was allowed. The more I trusted him, the more I was willing to let him roam. Eventually, I came to understand, through my own thick head, that I could learn as much from this lesson as Exley. Obedience is an important thing. Whether it's your dog, you, or those you live and work with— obedience can be freeing. But of course I think that was the hardest lesson in the whole world for me to learn.

I—like many, I suspect—am a hardheaded SOB. Although I have been able to change somewhat, thanks in no small part to Exley. If you told me what you wanted me to do, I was certain to go in a different direction. If you told me what not to do, I would go out and do exactly that. If you gave me life advice, career advice, love life advice, I was sure to spurn it. For many at home, work, or play, I was always an obstinate pain in the butt.

Strangely, one of the few places I never failed to do as told was football (although I would think my high school football coach might chuckle at this). But whether or not I failed at what I was supposed to do, I had every intention of trying my best. But why? Why in football (and, earlier in life, in baseball) would I actually listen? Because I was part of a team. And I knew if I didn't do what was required, if we all didn't do what was required, then the play and the team would fail. Why was I not able to take this lesson and apply it to life? Why did it take Exley's example to make this happen?

Ian Dunbar, PhD, a vet who is one of the great dog behaviorists of his generation, put it best when he wrote, "A well-trained, well-behaved, and good-natured puppy dog is always a joy to live with, but an untrained and uncivilized dog can be a perpetual nightmare."

Let's be honest—have you ever spent a day with someone who has an untrained dog? Their dog jumps on you when they greet you at the door, they harass you throughout your visit, they beg at the table, they may relieve themselves in the house (and if they do, the home you're visiting may smell none too pleasant), they are constantly barking, and they might show other kinds of unpleasant behavior.

Either these owners are constantly hollering at their canine family member, or they are on the brink of abusing it. What kind of life is that? We have all come out of one home or another or known of a dog in our neighborhood, and instead of being angry at the dog, we are angry at the owners, and we mumble, "Poor dog." We've all seen it.

Going to a home or meeting someone on the street who has a well-trained dog is a treat. For many years, before my dog-loving, well-intentioned mother-in-law ruined them for good by feeding them from the table during one of her visits, Exley and a newer addition to our family, Chelsea, were very good about not begging at the table during family events or dinner parties. Our friends were amazed and at times envious. A well-trained dog does not harass guests or people you meet on the street. They sit and stay, and they heel, not pull, and are, in general, a pleasure to be with.

Similarly, you've gone to visit friends who have children, or they've visited you. Children who are not obedient or who have not been taught to be obedient are difficult to put up with. They scream, destroy things, and make a playdate a horror show. There is nothing worse than being trapped with someone's ill-mannered children. As a parent, you forbid either that child or those children from coming over again or your child from visiting them.

As Dunbar points out, not only are you doing yourself a disservice, you are doing the dog a disservice. "Deny the dog an education, and she will not have the opportunity to fulfill her own canine potential; neither will she have the ability to communicate effectively with her human companions." In other words, if you fail to help train your dog, you are failing her in giving her a chance to be obedient. One of the keys to obedience is being as clear as you can about what you want. Only then can your dog give you what you want.

||||||||||||||||||||||||

The lesson that Exley taught me was that obedience is a freeing thing for you, for your dog, for your family, and for your career. The 19th-century British critic and social theorist John Ruskin wrote, "Freedom is only granted us that obedience may be more perfect." Obedience is about trust—trusting the one who is asking you to obey. It is also about the trust placed in you. If you don't trust a person, then you're with the wrong people, and you need to reevaluate yourself and your goals.

It wasn't long before I applied these principles beyond the fields and pathways of Prospect Park to good success. At work, I asked what my company wanted of me. Tell me what you want me to do, and I will do it. This was the most open I had ever let myself be, outside of sports. My boss told me what he wanted me to do. What lines I needed to take over to make things happen, and of course, what kinds of projects to look for as part of my job as an editor. With each success, I was allowed a little more freedom and was accorded a little more respect and leeway. By listening to my boss and giving him what he wanted, he gave me what I wanted—freedom. The more he trusted me to go out and buy what he wanted for our company, the more freedom he accorded me. I made his life easier. And when you make your boss's life easier, you are a very valuable commodity. And when our company was bought by Simon & Schuster, I was promoted and moved over to them. It was a great moment for me.

As I moved from job to job, I learned to fulfill my boss's desires first, and then I would be allowed the freedom I wanted, to work on more things.

MEET THE PARENTS

Unfortunately, while I was applying this lesson at the office, it was lost on me in my personal life. My longtime girlfriend and I had fallen through what had developed into thin ice. We had changed a lot while we were with each other over an on-and-off $4\frac{1}{2}$-year relationship. Either we were going to get married, or we were going to separate. We separated.

If obedience and trust are interlinked, it was apparent neither of us was being faithful to the relationship. Again, we're not talking about fidelity; we're talking about being supportive and loving, and trusting that each of us would be there for the other. Unlike our life with dogs, there are no natural training leads in our personal relationships. Either that tie exists, and it remains strong, or two people start to drift apart.

I think both of us wanted out, but it was very hard. We thought, especially when we moved to Brooklyn, that the next step was marriage. Instead, she found an apartment around the corner, and I was faced with the prospect of having to move home A friend watched Exley while she moved out. I remember the first night I came home to an empty apartment. In the entire living room and dining room, a large expanse, sat only a carpet and a television on a box. Exley and I had to lie down on the floor to watch television, because the furniture had been hers. Exley slept with me on the bed that night. I was pretty choked up and depressed in the empty bedroom. My professional life, which had seemed such a struggle, was finally turning the corner, but my personal life had hit the rocks.

I was low on money and was unlucky in finding a new apartment. I moved to New Jersey with my father, Phil, my stepmother, Joanne, and my sister, Leigh. I found it embarrassing. My dad was jovial and loud about the whole thing. He needled me, but he was also supportive.

Exley was a hound. There's a lot of hound in German shorthair pointers. And hounds love to sleep on elevated spots. And more than anything, like any dog, Exley loved the sofa. But my stepmother did not like Exley's preferences for her good furniture. Joanne kept her house immaculate. You truly could eat off the floors. And she hated that Exley slept on the couch.

Exley would be happily sleeping on the sofa, and when she came home from work or shopping—he knew her motor—he would jump off. She would come in, feel the cushions, see some hair on them, and freak! More than once, I found her chasing him around the house with a broom.

Eventually, Exley relented. He seemed to find enough places to sleep to make up for his love of Joanne's couches. She had a good sense of humor about it in the end, but it proved hard in the beginning. Exley finally learned to obey and was welcomed in his temporary home.

While he had reached an uneven truce with Joanne, Exley had found an enormous friend and supporter in my father. Phil loved Exley and saw in him his old dog, Timothy. They were fast and good friends. "Hey there, fella!" Phil's voice boomed. "You are one beautiful son of a gun. Come here, fella!" he said. Phil put out his big paw, and Exley immediately warmed to him. Regardless of my embarrassing predicament, it was good to know that my dad was so enthusiastic about Exley. I knew that if I was not around, Exley would find a bigger-than-life friend in my father.

||||||||||||||||||||||||

While living with my parents at the age of 30 was humiliating enough, the failure of my relationship was even more depressing. The reality of it was this: Dogs who fail to heed the lessons they've been taught become a burden to their families and to other dogs. People are very much in the same boat. And worse, in many cases, ill-behaved dogs, and people, are given up on; just look at the overcrowded animal shelters—and the personal ads. It is a failure on both sides, but it is a tragedy nonetheless.

I lay on my bed, in my parents' house, with Exley lying next to me, panting, looking at me. We all date a number of people. Relationships end. But I also had to be honest with myself. When it came to my intimate relationships—was it really me? Was I the disobedient, unsocialized dog no one wanted? Maybe I wasn't any better than Exley. Maybe I was just as hard to handle in relationships as I was at work. I always joked around that I was never going to get married. But I had met a number of nice women. I was critical, and I was also probably not a great boyfriend.

Exley was a great comfort and a good friend, but he was not a substitute for a girlfriend. I needed to do some work on myself. If Exley could become obedient and find a home, then maybe there was hope for me. I was soon to find out that I was about to meet the second-biggest challenge of my life, after Exley.

SECRETS TO REMEMBER

- Obedient dogs are happier dogs. They know what their human companions want from them and understand what they need to do to please you.

- Obedience is freeing. The more obedient you are, the higher the probability that you will gain more freedom.

- Obedience is about trust. That person trusts you, and you trust them. This kind of obedience is what binds us.

- Dogs, children, spouses, and workers who are not obedient are difficult and annoying, cause distress in their respective environments, and are generally avoided by others.

5 IT'S THE SIMPLE THINGS IN LIFE

"Man is an over-complicated organism.
If he is doomed to extinction,
he will die out for want of simplicity."
—*Ezra Pound, American Poet*

BOY MEETS GIRL

I lived with my parents for almost 5 embarrassing, excruciating, exhausting months. They didn't seem to mind so much. But I was 30 years old, and had been living on my own for almost 9 years when I moved home. I was going out on dates with women who were also in their thirties, trying desperately to hide the fact that I was living at home. Thirty and living at home? What a loser!

It was 5 or 6 months later when Nancy Campbell, the same woman who had matched me with Exley, called and told me about a great young dog editor who had just photographed her dogs for a story she was doing and that I had to meet her. I declined. I wasn't sure where I was going at the time. This editor subsequently went to work at Howell, where yet two more friends insisted that I meet her. I resisted both entreaties.

Then one day, I went to have lunch with a friend of mine. I was taking a summer Friday off, so I showed up at his office in a white polo shirt and a pair of orange hiking shorts. As we went down to lunch, who should get on the elevator but a short, cute, dark-haired young woman. My friend turned to me and said, "Oh, you two should meet. Carlo, this is Dominique; she's a new editor. Carlo works at Simon & Schuster."

She was cute. She was small and thin, with short brown hair and brown eyes. I called her once or twice, and we agreed on a lunch date. I remember I wasn't bowled over. I was still skeptical. I said to someone at my office, "I'm going out for a quick lunch. I'll be back in 45 minutes." We met for lunch at 12:30, and I got back to work at 4:30. I explained to my boss I had been in several other departments, following up on different issues. Whew!

Dominique was a tantalizing combination of attractive and tough. Her favorite movie was *The Sound of Music,* and the people she admired most were triathletes. She was a runner and belonged to the New York City Runner's Club. She was also an equestrian who had been raised on a small farm on the Philadelphia Main Line. She road to hounds, and could, when antagonized, curse like a sailor. She could muck out a stall and drink a pint of Guinness with the best of them. And she had a stubborn streak a mile long.

She liked me, even though I was this big loser living in Jersey with his parents. Eventually, I moved back to Brooklyn, and she moved in. In the beginning, Exley only heeded me. It was a nice rush for my ego, but a bad position for Exley to take with this new person in my life. It made life tense sometimes. I was angry at him for being obstinate when it came to her, and I wanted her to let up on him. The more she pressed, the more intensely I protected him. Eventually, he understood that he'd better pay her some mind, and they made their peace. Dominique and I were married 9 months later. We have now been married 10 years.

When we got married, I didn't even have a job.

IF YOU ARE NOT FIRED BY ENTHUSIASM, YOU WILL BE FIRED WITH ENTHUSIASM

To say it had been a horrible day was an understatement. My stay at Simon & Schuster had been brief and unrewarding. I had not been happy there, nor had they been happy with me. And sure enough, my time there came to an end.

On my last day, I packed up my Rolodex and my notebooks and personal papers and took what seemed like history's longest subway ride home. A lifelong dream of making it at a place like S & S had gone down the drain. It seemed on the train home that my career was an absolute train wreck.

Exley had developed a habit in the months earlier where he liked to carry things in his mouth. I had bought him a teddy bear, and being a natural retriever, he liked to carry the bear around. He never chewed on it. But whenever we came home, he brought us a present—most likely his teddy bear.

When I got home that day, Exley was there to greet me. He was wagging his tail and holding in his mouth his grungy, dirty teddy bear. I patted him on the head, and he pranced away very happy. He then carefully laid down the bear (as he always did) and began chirping away, eager to go outside and play. I certainly didn't feel like it. I just felt like crawling into some dark space and disappearing.

But Exley could be convincing, and we took a walk around the park. Exley played excitedly with friends and roamed happily. He was especially excited to play catch and retrieved the ball with incredible gusto. When we went home, he ate robustly and then came up on the couch and gave me numerous kisses. He lay down, with his head on my lap, as I drained a beer and watched television.

The next day, we did it all over again. Dominique was supportive, and I was very grateful. She married me when I had no job. But I cannot lie—it was Exley who pulled me out of the doldrums. Each day, we played and walked, and my spirits were picked up each time we took to the park.

Things got pretty rough during this period. I got very depressed. I had always thought it would be nice to have the summer off, but I despised it and did not enjoy my time "on the beach," as a friend liked to say. One thing about the publishing business in New York is, once you're out, it's hard to get back in. Once you step out of the working world, it's all too easy for former colleagues to forget to return your call or recommend you for an opening. The great thing about spending time with Exley was that his love was bottomless and unconditional. Did he care that I didn't have a job? Of course—he loved it! It just meant that I was around more often for walks and play. Now that's a pal.

The sad part was, here I was every day, walking in the woods in summer, going on adventures, and I was completely miserable. I didn't enjoy too much of the summer, other than my walks with Exley. Those walks were a way of getting away. Otherwise, I was consumed with getting a job and becoming someone again. Here I was, with so much time on my hands, and I couldn't enjoy myself.

By end of August and early September, I had hit rock

bottom. My unemployment ran out. It got to the point where I was willing to take anything—anything. At one point, I applied to Macy's for an executive position and for a job as a Santa Claus. When Macy's called, the kind human resources person asked if I would like to come in for an interview. I said I would. I was pleasant, professional, and courteous. She set a date and time for my interview and was about to hang up.

"Excuse me," I said. "Which position is this for?"

"Which one did you sign up for?" she asked warily.

"No, I asked first," I said, worried.

"Executive program?"

"Great!" I said happily. "Have a nice day, and thank you!" and hung up the phone. My stories of my time at Macy's are a whole other book. It was a surreal experience. I trained upstairs in toys for 3 weeks, but after that, they called me to the store manager's office. I had sold shirts and ties for 2½ years before getting into the publishing business. Macy's was going to put that experience to good use. Three weeks in, and my first day downstairs was the day after Thanksgiving—Black Friday. I arrived at 7:00 a.m., pressing my way between 2,000 people who were waiting to get in. I spent countless hours over the next 12 months, dressed in a double-breasted pinstripe suit, black wingtips, English spread collar, and Italian silk tie, climbing the shelves of the dusty stockrooms, trying to find odd sizes like 15 ½ neck 36 sleeve, and 18 neck 32 sleeve—or telling customers "No, only in the French blue, not the powder blue."

And every day, I walked Exley in the morning and the evening. I worked weekends and saw my wife on weeknights. I spent countless weekday mornings and afternoons walking Exley in the park. The routine of our everyday lives was both a grind and a blessing. The grind drove me crazy, especially when I was dying for something better. But it was keeping up with the grind that kept me from losing my mind.

Exley and I had many a long walk on a nice morning or afternoon when none of our other dog friends were around. We played a game of fetch or tug-of-war. It was kind of comical. Together, we learned a new trick. I finally got Exley to do a long stay. I could walk 100 yards away, and he stayed until I called him, no matter what was going on. It was an Olympic moment in our lives—well, my life. The second time we executed it, instead of coming back to me, Exley chased a squirrel. But he stayed until I released him. Even if my career was stalled, I could still accomplish *something* with Exley.

On our way home, as usual, I stopped and bought two bagels, a cup of coffee, and the paper. I fed him a bagel while I had mine with coffee, and then we went home, and I fed him a more nutritious breakfast. He was company, and he was good company. He took my mind off things, especially when I was down. He was a clown, a complicated kid, and a dog all rolled into one.

"Remember, there's no such thing as a small act of kindness. Every act creates a ripple with no logical end," wrote *Dilbert* creator Scott Adams. It certainly was true between Exley and me.

I was miserable, but I can't begin to explain the value of those walks and the time he and I spent together and how it healed me. A simple walk. A simple show of affection. These were the things that helped me weather an emotional time in my life.

I don't know if it has ever been scientifically proven, but anyone with a dog knows how incredibly empathetic dogs are. Exley made an extra effort to lift my spirits. If we could all be that straightforward with our affection, the world would be a better place. Sometimes, it seems to me, looking back, those simple moments of connection that I've often overlooked at their occurrence are really my most valuable possessions. I count those memories like so many valuable baubles in a jewelry box. From time to time, I take them out to examine them, to smile at the facets and cuts and the shimmering beauty and bask in their radiance. Many of those flickering memories include Exley.

IT'S A GIRL!

Eventually, Dominique and I, and Exley, moved to New Jersey. We bought an old Victorian house, from the 1890s, gray with blue shutters and white gingerbread, with the thought of filling it up with kids. We wanted lots of kids. But before we got busy making babies, we decided to bring home a friend for Exley. And so Chelsea joined us as our German shepherd. We adopted Chelsea quite by accident from a local animal shelter. We were looking for a female Lab or golden retriever as a companion for Exley, because we wanted another sporting dog who was stocky and strong. Exley could be quite exuberant during play, and we needed a companion who could give as good as she got and who would not be intimidated by his rather physical ways.

We'd seen a beautiful Yellow Lab, and we thought she would make an excellent companion. She was lovable and friendly, with a beautiful face and sturdy build. So we decided to bring Exley to the shelter, place the two in a large fenced-in pen the size of a decent backyard, and make sure that they got along. We brought the retriever into the pen. As soon as she saw Exley, who at the time was watering the fence posts and completely uninterested, she went mad, barking, gnashing her teeth, and snarling, so much so that small bits of foam started flying from her mouth. That was the end of that.

We decided, since we were at the shelter with Exley, that we might as well see if there was any other dog we liked. It wasn't long before we saw this beautiful white German shepherd. She was very shy and sitting at the back of her pen. As wolflike as she appeared, she was actually timid and leery. She was extremely affectionate and very friendly. She was 5 years old and had been owned by an older woman who had to give her up when she was forced to move into assisted living. While she later proved to be very leery of all men (which shows you how smart she was), she warmed to me instantly. We introduced her to Exley, and the two were quite compatible. And that was how Chelsea came into our lives.

However, Chelsea's true colors came out later in the week, when she proved more than a match for Exley. He now had a competitor who would take no guff. While he was used to being a bully in many situations, he had a new 85-pound play-mate who was easily his physical and mental equal. It was an alpha male and an alpha bitch. For the 7 years they were together, they hip-checked each other into doorways and cabinets at every turn, raced each other, barking, to the door, stole each other's food, wrestled intensely, fought over sleeping spots, toys, and just about everything. It never came to biting. I've always believed, as Matt Weinstein and Luke

Barber entitled their book, *Dogs Don't Bite When a Growl Will Do*. But they also became great friends and certainly partners in crime.

During Chelsea's first week in our home, we had my parents Phil and Joanne over for a late-lunch, early-dinner. We were making a London broil. I was showing my parents something upstairs when we heard Dominique screaming, "NO!!! No!! Noooooooo!!!" I immediately checked the room we were in, and there was Exley with his ears perked up. I was greatly relieved to see him there instead of getting hollered at downstairs. Then I realized it must be Chelsea who had done something wrong.

We all raced downstairs, chuckling among ourselves, because we knew something bad had happened. Chelsea had stolen our 8-pound piece of beef from the counter and started noshing on it under the kitchen table. Secretly, I was thrilled. Now we knew we had a dog who was equal to Exley and that he would not be the sole participant in any further mischief. While we all want our dogs to be model citizens, and we all shell out money on training books, deep down inside we hope that our dogs will exhibit some small amount of spirit and independence. While I was none too pleased about having to run out for a new roast, I admired Chelsea's pluck.

THE BONE

It was a rainy late-winter day. One of those raw days when the sky is perpetually gray and the ground wet, and it just seems cold no matter whether you are in the house or outside. Dominique was at work, and I was home sick with a cold. It was just me and the dogs hanging around the house.

I tried to go back to bed after the early-morning routine, but I was soon bored and walked around the house, half in street clothes and half in pajamas. Chelsea was asleep under the kitchen table. As I paced the house, Exley followed in tow. He was starting to get on my nerves, when his nose suddenly went up into the air. He smelled something.

The last time I had seen him do this, he went on point in our kitchen in Brooklyn. His body absolutely rigid. It turned out we had mice.

While he and I were standing in the den, I could see he didn't have it quite yet. He sniffed the air, his nose up. He was catching a whiff, but he wasn't sure where it was coming from. Although this momentarily broke the spell of boredom, I eventually ignored him and sat on the couch and watched television. I dozed on and off.

I dreamed of my wife and the dogs. I dreamed of walking the fields with Exley and Chelsea. And I dreamed he had cornered something in the field. He was whining and yapping, and I kept trying to call him off. He kept whining, scratching at the ground, and yapping, and I kept calling him to me.

Exley let out a loud bark, and I shot up off the couch. He paid me little mind. He was barking at the bottom of the couch where I had fallen asleep. It was he who had been barking and yapping the whole time. His face was intent, his ears alert, his gaze fixed. The muscles on his body rippled. It was a happy intent, as his little tail was fanning back and forth. He let out a loud bark again. I was only hoping it wasn't another mouse.

Enough was enough. I had to get up. I got on my hands and knees and saw under the couch a large marrow bone covered in dust and cobwebs.

"This? This is what all the commotion is about?!" I hollered. I stretched and strained, finally reaching the grotesque piece of putrid bone, long since forgotten under the sofa. "This is what you woke me up for?!" I groaned. Exley stared at my hand as if he'd been searching his whole life for this forgotten treat. I tossed the 6-inch-long section of cow femur to the floor. Exhausted, I sank into the sofa after the bone hit the floor with a loud "thunk!"

Exley attacked the bone as if it were fresh meat. His eyes were always filled with expression. His brown furry eyebrows twitched, one higher than the other, with excitement. Then his eyes widened, with a look almost like shock, as I offered it to him. He picked it up and looked happily at me, circled three

times, and settled down. He folded his paws over the filthy, dried-out bone and dug in, grinding against it like a carpenter with a planer.

I fell asleep again. At three o'clock, Exley was still at it. I made some phone calls, padded around the house, and watched a movie, and the whole time, Exley ground his teeth against that old bone. Later, my wife came home, we ate, she told me about her day, and she fed the dogs.

I was shocked. Exley gave up the bone, walked into the kitchen, ate quickly, and then happily trotted back to the den to work on his bone. He gnawed on the thing through all of our nighttime television watching. We let the dogs out and then made our way upstairs for bedtime. Unknown to me, Exley carried his bone up with us. We went to bed and turned out the lights. As we began to nestle in, I heard a strange sound in the darkness. As my ears focused in, I realized that Exley was at it again.

"Exley! No!" I shot up in a flash. I found the bone and placed it on top of our dresser. By now it was only about $2\frac{1}{2}$ inches long and dripping with dog spit. Exley whined and cried.

We tossed and turned some, and I hollered at him. Finally, he circled three times and sank into his dog bed—and let out a big, disgruntled groan and then a long sigh. The message was crystal clear.

The next morning was unique. Exley was asleep when we arose, which hardly ever happened. He was the last one to get up. He did not forget his bone, but we decided it was better off thrown in the trash. He was heartbroken, of course. When it came time for breakfast, I noticed something. There was something wrong with Exley's teeth. Or should I say tooth?

One of his bottom fangs was suddenly shorter than the other. Perceptibly shorter. He had worn down one of his teeth on this bone! It was a mark on his canine profile that time would not change. This experience did not diminish his love of bones. He returned to the couch many times thereafter, and from time to time, he found treats there and elsewhere.

I couldn't help but envy the intensity of Exley's discovery. Here I was, bored all day, when I could have made my own discoveries. Had I wasted an opportunity? While I'm continually bombarded 24/7 by new products or distractions, what are the simple objects that I've overlooked that might keep me busy all day long—something simple but worth obsessing over—worth doing perfectly?

THE BOWL OF MACERATED FRUIT

I was at Macy's for an eternity—13 to 14 colorful months. McGraw-Hill eventually rescued me. I managed four book clubs in their book club division. As I eased into my mid- to late thirties, I hit the most industrious patch in my professional life. I was writing a book a year. My wife joined several local groups, including the running club. We had settled nicely into our suburban life. But children hadn't yet entered our lives.

I was in Toronto in January. Along with three other executives, I had just come from a sales conference and stood in the airport, waiting for the plane to board. Phoning home, I envisioned returning to my wife, my dogs, and my cozy little circa–1895 Victorian house. It was six o'clock, and I was exhausted. The phone rang, and then a shrill voice answered. I had to jerk the receiver away from my ear.

"The damn dog has just destroyed the entire house. I had to throw out the rug in the den. I had to mop up the kitchen, the den, and the walls! I had no money and had to raid the change jar 'cause we had no paper towels, and you have the cash card for the savings account, and checking is broke! You better get here fast. When are you getting home?"

I stammered, "I haven't boarded yet."

"Haven't boarded yet?!" Dominique shrieked. "Well, I'm

not doing another thing. When you get home, you can take care of it!" I tried to calm her down, but the conversation took a decidedly downward turn despite my best efforts. She told me the whole sordid story. We hung up, and a massive knot immediately developed in the pit of my stomach. I glumly headed for the gate, dreading the flight home.

During the Christmas of 1998, my father-in-law's longtime companion, Fran, made a lovely winter compote, complete with peaches, cherries, plums, port, brandy, and red wine. It was an elegant concoction, and she had made almost a gallon for us that sat on our kitchen table in a lovely giant antique glass jar. As we'd been home the whole time between Christmas and New Year, the dogs had never really discovered or cared about the contents. Or so we thought.

Apparently, Exley, a sometime drinker of potent beverages (he liked to sample mixed drinks left on coffee tables during cocktail parties) had been eyeing the booty-laden jar, awaiting the right opportunity. It took him only 2 days with us back at work before he struck. It was classic Exley.

He started by knocking the jar off the table, emptying its rich contents on the kitchen floor. He ate all the fruit and drank most of the nectar without cutting himself. Our other dog, Chelsea, did not participate. Having had his fill, Exley then proceeded in reverse. He dispensed the compote back into our house from both ends—front and back. In a scene inspired by Jackson Pollock, he decorated the rugs, floors, and walls with the results of his misdeed. Few objects had been spared. The undersides of the floorboards, which could be seen from the basement, were drenched with this mixture of fruit-laden alcohol and excrement. Sometime after the incident, I secretly did the best I could to clean up down there, because my wife didn't know. I guess now she does.

Dominique had come home to this horrendous scene only to find that she could not clean up, because we had no paper towels and no money in the checking account to buy any. She had to collect coins out of our change jar, drive to the store, come back, and then begin the gruesome job of cleaning up. She threw the dog onto the deck behind the house. He proceeded to walk in circles and eventually tipped over into a small bed of leaves that had collected in the corner of the deck. She called animal poison control, but they said at that point, there was nothing she could do except make sure he had enough water. She threw a dish of water at him.

For anyone who has ever lived near or had to pass a water filtration plant or sewage plant, the moment is telling. When you pass one of these on the highway, you can sometimes smell it for miles. Or when you lay down fresh manure on a farm in the heat of a humid summer. It's enough to make you gag. That was what this smelled like. But this was the perfume—not the aftershave. It hit me like smelling salts. And this was with all the kitchen windows wide open at 11 or 12 at night, hours after my poor wife had cleaned up.

And there, by the kitchen table, was Exley, curled up in a ball on his stained and smelly dog bed, in the fetal position. He lifted his head, looked up at me with his big, soulful brown eyes, and wagged his tail. Then his eyes rolled backward as he himself rolled over and flopped onto his other side on the floor with a thud. He didn't move, except for the rise and fall of his chest. Some wind escaping from his hindquarters was the only other acknowledgment of my long-awaited homecoming. The only thing colder that night than the kitchen in our house was the space between my wife and me in our bed. It would be months before she was able to laugh about it.

The next morning, I was greeted in the same way I always was. Exley, who had knocked down the kitchen gate, pranced around our bedroom in the predawn, licking my face with his bootlegger's bar-rag bad breath. He was still solidly built. The only sign of age on his face was a small white ring that was sneaking its way around his big chocolate brown snout. But the rest of him seemed fine. He wanted to go outside. His gait was normal, and he was completely unfazed.

SIMPLICITY

By this time, we were fairly good friends with many people around the neighborhood. Childless, we often had dinner parties, cookouts, cocktail parties. Whatever. Life became quite hectic. We both were working hard, Dominique at her publishing company and I at mine. We hired a walker for the dogs during the day. We finally had some money in the bank and good friends. I kept pressing, because I was afraid at one point, it would all stop.

One night, we had some people over, and we were just hanging out. I was making mention of some far-flung idea. I am sure it was preposterous. It was probably the beer or the wine talking—maybe both. I said something, and then one of my dinner companions almost choked on whatever she was drinking.

She snorted. "Ah, right, like you would ever take time off to do that! Admit it—you're a workaholic!" I was hurt. My wife looked at me, and then looked away, and walked into the kitchen.

Had I been ignoring my wife? I knew she was more irritable than before. We had argued about me taking on too much work. But now it occurred to me as never before. Was I placing the work between us? Maybe I was.

I had been working hard, achieving, for both of us—for me and her. She had married me when I had no job, and I wanted so much to prove to her that I could provide. I was at a crossroads where I was letting the complicated overwhelm the simple. I was so happy that my career was finally taking shape that I hadn't paid enough attention to life at home. Coming back from that business trip and coming to the realization that perhaps I wasn't home enough, I knew it was time to turn a corner.

When I was younger, I used to think that people who traveled the world and had read a great deal were the wisest. I realize now that I was mistaking information for wisdom. As I've grown older, I've found more often than not that the wisest people are usually not the ones you think they are. Sometimes, it's someone who really hasn't gone anywhere but who knows one place very, very well.

There is no way I would tell you that this is the first anyone has ever written about simplicity and the value of simple things. A forest of trees has been slain to describe the value of such thoughts. But Exley, his lifestyle and his wants and desires, reminded me more often than not that it was the simple things, like enjoying snowfall, going for a walk, lying in the sun, and sleeping on the couch, that were the secrets to what was valuable. With Dominique (and Exley), sometimes a walk in the woods on a sunny morning was as good a thing as I could ever have.

The world was turning from my twenties, when it seemed I could hardly find two dimes to rub together, to my thirties, when I had a few dollars in the bank and we could afford a real vacation now and again. Sure, we had credit card bills and car payments, but who doesn't? As we juggled our personal and professional lives, time started moving faster and faster. And though I didn't know it, life was about to go a little faster.

But there were times when I was able to slow the picture down some. Mostly, those days started the way they had when I was younger. I would take Exley for a walk in the woods, or play a game of fetch or tug-of-war. Maybe there was a job I needed to do around the house—something simple that needed to be obsessed over and done perfectly. Or maybe it was just spending a Saturday or Sunday laid up on the couch. I was hanging out with my friend. Exley was trying to teach me to catch my breath.

Famed novelist Milan Kundera wrote, "Dogs are our link to paradise. . . . To sit with a dog on a hillside on a glorious afternoon is to be back in Eden, where doing nothing was not boring—it was peace." What I wanted was success; but what I needed was peace. And peace is a lot harder to come by. I needed to slow down, but sometimes the only way I could remember to do it was by listening to my dog.

SECRETS TO REMEMBER

- Simplicity is the stripping away of the things that occupy us instead of what make us whole.

- Enjoying the simple things—a bone, a burger, an afternoon on a hammock—is essential. It helps ground you.

- Everyone—including you and your dog—needs time to recharge.

- Dogs, children, spouses, coworkers, and employees need time to lean back and smell the roses. Always make sure that you and your coworkers and employees take all their vacation time. Someone who doesn't is telling you something about themselves.

6 SIMPLE ACTS OF KINDNESS ARE THE BEST ACTS

"The best portion of a good man's life,
His little, nameless, unremembered acts,
Of kindness and of love."
—*William Wordsworth*

The one thing all dog owners can relate to is the unbelievable amount of unconditional love a dog offers. No matter your mood, no matter the circumstances, a dog's unconditional love is the greatest spirit lifter. Dogs always greet you at the door enthusiastically. Whether you went outside for only a moment, or you've been away a week, your return is hailed as a great triumph. Give most dogs a chance, and they will shower you with kisses. These are simple acts of kindness that no bauble, no trinket can quite match. We would all be better off if we followed their example.

SHARING A BED

Back in our bachelor days, I let Exley sleep up on the bed. He started by sleeping curled up at the bottom of the bed. Then, during the subsequent months, he slowly crept up toward the top. I knew I was being way too nice, and Nancy Campbell, my shorthair mentor, would have been very angry. "You need to be the alpha male," her voice echoed in my brain. "You can't be his friend. If you won't take control, he will. He wants to be the alpha male . . . especially if he sees you as an equal."

I realized I should have heeded this voice when I awoke one morning to find Exley, his head next to mine on the pillow, snoring away.

On one particularly hot night back in Brooklyn, I was tossing and turning in bed. I was sweating like I was on a treadmill. It was one of those miserable New York summer nights. Exley was on the bed with me. And every time I awoke, he was lying pressed against me. First at 1:20 a.m., and then at 1:45 a.m., and again at 2:15 a.m. "Do you know how hot it is?" I growled. I pushed him away, tossed, turned, and fell asleep. Fifteen minutes later, he was back up against me again. This continued for half the night. Finally exasperated at 3:30 a.m., I lost my temper and screamed at him.

"Do you not get it? It's hot!" I hollered. Numerous obscenities flew from my mouth into the hot night air. I pulled Exley by the collar and flung him off the bed. "You hard-headed . . . ugh. Down!" I screamed. "DOWN!" Exley bowed his head, gave me a sad look, twirled three times, and finally flopped down on the floor. He let out a big sigh and then a long groan. I continued to curse him and rolled over to go to sleep.

I tossed and turned a few more times. I think it was some time around 4:00 a.m. when I finally woke up and went to sleep for the last time. When I awoke, I was curled in a ball, and when I opened my eyes, there on the pillow across from mine was Exley. He was lying against me. I was still a little mad but mostly bemused. Knowing Exley, yes, he was hardheaded, but his desire to be close to me was far ahead of just sharing the bed. And for that, how could you not like him?

Of course, when I got married, Exley soon lost his place on the bed. It was a difficult transition for the dog, but it was the correct order of things. Still, how could you not remember and reward such devotion?

TREATS CAN BE TRICKS

Dominique had a great idea that was both a noble gesture and a smart solution to a problem. She and I both worked. Each day, we left the house in the morning, a dog walker visited in the early afternoon, and we returned home by dinnertime.

But when we prepared to leave in the morning, the dogs became anxious. There was whining from both Exley (who was a constant whiner) and Chelsea (who was normally a groaner). Obviously, our puppies were suffering from separation anxiety.

Dominique talked to several dog-training professionals, and one of them suggested giving the dogs a treat every time we left the house. The idea was to distract Exley and Chelsea from fretting. On short trips, we gave them a few dog biscuits. During the week, we gave them frozen marrow bones or long bones filled with peanut butter. These lasted a few hours. Exley did his little circle dance every time Dominique or I reached into the freezer for the beloved marrow bones.

It wasn't long before the dogs started to anticipate our departure in a different way—they began looking forward to it. This simple act turned a sad farewell into a happy moment for us all.

KISSES FOR MY FAVORITE GIRL

Bizarre as it might seem, at one point, we had only one dog bed upstairs in our bedroom. And whoever got up to the bedroom first got the bed. There was lots of whining, moaning, and groaning, and sometimes the early leader gave up—and sometimes not. But Exley had a routine that always, always, always worked on Chelsea. And it was a great life lesson.

One night, Chelsea was the first to go upstairs and sat atop the dog bed in all her white shepherd glory. And she groaned when Exley entered, because she knew he considered the bed his domain. He stood over her a bit, and she groaned. He whined. She growled, and he walked away. But he was only biding his time. He waited 5 minutes and then tried again. This went on several times. And then he came back and threw the coup de grâce.

Exley lovingly approached her and began nuzzling her. He licked her face and nuzzled her ear. Chelsea groaned with happiness, and she eventually rolled over on her back in submission, ready for more nuzzling and love play. Exley then moved into the vacated spot immediately and curled up in a ball. Game over.

This scene played itself out many times. Maybe it was just Chelsea's way of getting affection from him—who knows? Exley's little routine, as duplicitous as it was, was a perfect illustration of the old adage of catching more flies with sugar. Exley might have started a fight each time. He had a simple problem, and he developed a simple, though slightly underhanded, solution.

SOMETIMES IT'S SOMETHING SMALL

It's not always the big moments you remember most when you miss someone. More often than not, it's the small things. Some small, often overlooked, and seemingly insignificant detail that instantly brings a person or place to mind.

For example, when I see stairs, I often think of Exley. After we moved to Freehold, Exley and I had a ritual in which he would not go to bed until I did. Especially when I was busy commuting, Exley waited downstairs for me to return. He slept on the sofa, or sprawled out on the kitchen floor in summer, awaiting my late arrival home.

For example, when I reached the door, he came to me and greeted me happily, the filthy teddy bear in his mouth. It always brought me joy after a long day working and commuting to find Exley waiting for me. Then we began to ascend the staircase. He went first. He trudged halfway up the stairs and then turned around. He sat down, hindquarters on one step, front paws on another, and waited. As I began shutting off the lights, I eventually turned to the stairs, and there he was.

I joined Exley on the staircase and talked to him.

"Hey there, you hound. You waitin' for me?" I said. His tail started buzzing, and I chuckled. "Who's my big old puppy?

Who's my big old puppy?" He gave me a lick or two. He bowed his head into me like a puppy, nuzzling his slowly graying, big brown jowly snout into my chest. I would rub right behind his big, floppy brown ears and under his speckled chin. And we spent a minute. It was like he was a young boy trying to give me a hug. And then, slowly, he unwound, turned, and ascended the rest of the stairs. Off to bed.

Those simple moments. Those were special.

SIMPLE ACTS OF KINDNESS

The English novelist Aldous Huxley wrote, "To his dog, every man is Napoleon; hence the constant popularity of dogs." We all know he's right. The admiration and absolute devotion make dogs very popular. And we find comfort in them. Sometimes we take their friendship, their love, and their kindness for granted. But it was hard for me to learn this lesson. I did not understand the value of kindness. In the mayhem of modern life, I failed to understand the lesson of the dog. The thing that binds us is the exchange of everyday kindness.

At this point in my career, I was doing much better than when I first married Dominique. But the commute was tough and long. My grandmother Catherine De Vito decided to give up her home of 35 years and moved into an assisted-living apartment building. She had many new friends and an easier physical existence than she did padding around her four-bedroom house. Saddled with arthritis, this once formidable woman now struggled with the multiple stairs of her longtime home. Her new apartment was nice, but I think sometimes loneliness set in.

On my long rides home, I started calling her and other family members. I called just to say hello—nothing deep or long. She seemed to like it. She chatted, telling me current gossip and stories about the old days. I filled her in on the wife, the dogs, and my job. My aunt told me later that my grandmother told her she loved it when I called. It was only a 10-minute call, every other week or once a month. It was very little effort, but it meant a lot to her.

Looking back, I realize that the simple acts of kindness that I might perform were the real small miracles. This is one of the single most important tricks my dog taught me. Exley taught me about the possibilities, the power, the benefits of kindness. I was blind to it for a long time—and then sometimes forgetful of it. Exley reminded me that I wanted to be better, kinder. Sometimes, I only needed reminding. That's probably true about us all.

SECRETS TO REMEMBER

- Your dog is probably the kindest person you know.

- A simple act of kindness will do someone else good—and will endear you to them that much more.

- A simple act of kindness toward your spouse will go a long way to improving your relationship.

- Imagine what doing a small, nice thing for your parents or your kids would mean to them.

- No coworker or employer will ever think any less of you because you did something nice for someone you work with.

7 EVERY ONCE IN A WHILE, IT'S GOOD TO PLAY THE CLOWN

> "To make mistakes is human;
> to stumble is commonplace; to be able
> to laugh at yourself is maturity."
> —*William A. Ward*

Having a sense of humor is one of the most important things in life. Not taking yourself too seriously is another. Exley and dogs in general are an excellent foil for our tension and rigidity.

Exley's name on the American Kennel Club (AKC) register was Kingswood's Bring on the Clown. While the name pretty much says it all, I cherish the pictures I took of Exley over the years. Whether he was playing, running, or sometimes even posing, you could always see his clownish spirit. But there were two photos in particular I loved.

THE BIRTHDAY PARTY

The first photo was taken in our backyard on Broad Street, in Freehold. Our next-door neighbors, with whom we shared a fence line, Jim and Lia Prendergast, were having a birthday party for one of their daughters. They were always very kind, inviting us to such events. They had a large extended family, and it seemed every member attended each of these celebrations.

Jim, who made the best barbecued chicken I have ever had (and that's saying lots), grilled up enormous amounts of chicken, and there were plenty of sides, and a big fun, imaginative, homemade cake. The lawn was filled with lawn chairs, plastic tablecloths, bowls of potato chips, chests filled with iced drinks, and lots of children laughing and running around.

One year, while we all sang the birthday song, Exley joined in by whining at the fence, hoping to win a piece of cake. Someone, probably Dominique, put one of the children's birthday hats on Exley. Now usually, Exley shunned any adornment of his head. He would normally use his paws to pull it off.

But for some reason, with this colorful cone sitting atop his head, Exley was quite proud. He paraded up and down the fence, his big tongue hanging out, his head up, his ears perked, his gait bouncy. Jim and Lia and their guests laughed and guffawed. Dominique and I laughed too. He wore that hat for a good 10 to 15 minutes, running around the yard, doing his little circle dance, and barking and entreating the scampering children to come play with him. His eyes were bright, and he was clearly having as much fun as any of the guests.

And that is one of my favorite photos of Exley, prancing the length of the fence, bright-eyed and bouncy, parading in his birthday hat for all to see. I still don't know what he thought he was doing. But I know one thing—he was having fun. And he didn't care who was laughing at him or who was laughing with him.

THE FOLDING CHAIR

My brother-in-law Michael and his wife, Jill, gave us a set of canvas-backed, wooden folding director's chairs when we first moved to the suburbs as a housewarming gift. They were extremely handy, since they were useful outdoors as well as the fact that they matched our den, where we also used them from time to time.

One chair had been somewhat rickety from the start. And like most other men, I kept talking about fixing it every time I sat in it. I knew exactly what needed to be fixed. I knew what pieces I needed, what pieces I had on my workbench, and where to buy the ones I didn't have. In short, the chair was fixed, in my mind, at least two dozen times without my ever having to do anything.

"I thought you said you were going to fix that thing this weekend," Dominique would say.

"Don't nag. I hate nagging. I'll get it done. Didn't I tell you I was going to do it? I'll do it," I said with absolute resolve and a load of attitude thrown in. Of course, I never did. The chair wobbled and swayed a little more. And because I had gained a few pounds over the intervening years, it came to a point where I avoided the chair at all times.

One day, I came home from working at McGraw-Hill, and I was exhausted. I had dealt with a number of things, and I just wanted to fall onto the sofa and numb myself with whatever drivel was on television and just have a good laugh. Dominique was still in the kitchen, talking animatedly, when I slogged into the den, picked up the remote control, and clicked on the television.

The dogs were on the covered sofa. "Fine," I thought to myself. Without thinking, I threw myself into the canvas-backed director's chair. The thing swayed. I tried to right myself. Oh, no! I wasn't thinking. The chair and I swayed this way and that. I struggled to get up, but I could not find my legs as the chair swayed yet again. I tried to put weight on the arms of the chair to right myself.

It took maybe 10 seconds, but in my mind it seemed like it took 10 minutes. I felt like I was in one of those thousands of cartoons where the ice begins to crack, and the character on the ice looks down to the frozen floor beneath him in horror as the crack starts to multiply across the entire lake.

Suddenly, there was a small cracking sound—it lasted a second or two. It was quiet but just loud enough to let me know I was toast.

As the chair groaned, Exley and Chelsea looked up quickly. They were up in a shot, sitting on the couch, looking at me quizzically, as if to say, "What have you done? Why in the world are you sitting in that chair?!"

I tried to stagger to my feet, but the chair emitted a long, slow growl, and I could feel the strength of the chair in my palms begin to sink, and then a sudden "CRACK!"

The chair snapped in two, the arms flopped over in opposite directions, the seat fell through when the arms gave way, and I fell backward with a loud crash, my head almost landing in the kitchen.

All I could see was the ceiling—and then I heard my wife. "Oh my God!" she screamed. But my face was soon covered in dog kisses. It seemed Exley and Chelsea thought it was a game. They both jumped down and showered me with dog kisses. I was covered in dog spit. I began to laugh. At first, it was a small chuckle, but the more I tried to get up, the more the dogs were on top of me, trying to lick my face. The more I tried to turn away, the more they sought my face. I started laughing louder now. And as I giggled and laughed, Exley put his paw on my chest, as if to hold me down, while he licked me.

Instead of helping me up, once my wife saw that I was okay, rolling around in the remains of our old chair on the den floor, she ran into the kitchen and got the camera.

Now I started to guffaw. The dogs were trying all the harder to kiss me now, pressing down on my chest, while my wife took pictures of the three of us on the floor. One of these is my other favorite photo, and happily, it also includes Chelsea as well.

It took me forever to get up — the dogs thought it was such fun.

LUKE—I AM YOUR FATHER

In the late 1990s, I was an associate publisher working in Philadelphia. It was a new job with a lot of responsibility.

When *Star Wars Episode 1* was getting ready to premiere, my company was one of the licensees. As a licensee, I was required to go to Lucasfilm Ranch, in northern California, and read the script for the movie so we could produce the two books that we were publishing to coincide with the movie. I can't lie—

reading the script rekindled in me a fandom for the movies that were so popular in previous years.

Star Wars merchandise was, of course, still available in stores. And for some of our key accounts, we bought light sabers as gifts for buyers and merchandise managers. Now, as geeky as it sounds, I always liked light sabers. When the original movies came out, I was in my early twenties, too old and too cool to play with them.

Well into my late thirties, I could now buy a light saber (telling some clerk it was for a niece, nephew, or a son—which I did not have at the time) without looking like a nerd. So I bought some for our business associates, but I couldn't help buying a few for myself.

Dominique was sort of shocked. It confirmed for her, I think, the fact that I was truly nuts. And maybe I was. I loaded up the handles with batteries and then flicked the switch, commencing my transformation to Jedi Knight. The light went on as the plastic blade telescoped out. I thought it was really quite cool. My wife was horrified. Apparently, so was Exley.

As soon as I flicked it open, Exley started to whine and bark at the extended saber. I quickly pulled it up, and Exley leapt at it. It made no noise, and you could barely see the green light illuminating the tube. He freaked. I instantly had an idea.

That night, I invited Exley outside, which was never a hard

thing to do. At that point, I walked out to the middle of the backyard, called Exley over to me, and repeated the lines from the movie.

"Luke, I am your father," I said, wheezing, and imitating James Earl Jones's famous voice. "Join me, and together we can rule the universe as father and son." At this point, I switched on the light saber and snapped it to its full length. In the warm, dark spring night, Exley and I did royal battle. I did my best imitating the lines of Darth Vader, Obi-Wan Kenobi, and Luke Skywalker. I waved the glowing green saber through the dark night, and Exley whined, yelped, and barked, lunging at it with violent ferocity. Inexplicably, he absolutely reviled the saber and chased it with a fervor I cannot quite relate with words.

We would do battle for 10 to 15 minutes. My light saber technique emulated the solemnic movements of the original *Star Wars* movie, replaying moments of the second battle of Darth and Obi-Wan. At other times, I leapt from the deck and then worked my way back up the stairs, only to leap off again, à la Douglas Fairbanks, Jr. The game always ended when Exley finally caught the blade of the light saber in his mouth. Once this was accomplished, before I could stop him, he destroyed at least one portion of the saber, so that it was no longer able to function. He crunched it like he was chewing on a cow's leg.

It got to the point that when I came home with a new light saber, even while it was in the package, I would show it to him, and he would start whining and barking. He tried to snatch it from my hands. I placed it on top of the refrigerator or in a cabinet. He continued to whine for a minute or two, but then he'd let it go. Then, as night fell, I said to him, "Luke—I am your father." His head tilted, and his ears perked up, and his little tail started fanning back and forth.

After *Episode 1* came out, the toy companies introduced the two-bladed saber used by Darth Maul in the film. This was very exciting. I tried emulating the moves of the terrifying new character. Needless to say, I may have looked stupid, but Exley loved it. And when Exley caught one blade, we could then fight to the death with the second blade. He leapt and snarled, growled and snapped. It was always against the blade. He never threatened me once—not even by mistake. But he hated the light saber.

"The great pleasure of a dog is that you may make a fool of yourself with him," wrote the great British writer Samuel Butler, "and not only will he not scold you, he will make a fool of himself too." Many years later, I still think of those spring and summer nights spent in the small backyard of our first house in New Jersey, dueling in the dark, and both of us enjoying it immensely. Me spinning, laughing, and repeating the lines of the movies, and him whirling, twisting, and diving, trying to outdo me. It was such great fun.

THE TEARS OF A CLOWN

Dogs have no shame. They are funny, and they don't care if you laugh at them or with them. When you are happy, they are happy. I have found that it's important to have a sense of humor. I hope it makes me easier to be around. It sure made Exley easier to be around. And I have found, especially in my relationships with friends, family, and coworkers, that having a sense of humor, at the appropriate times, helps my relationships function a little more smoothly.

I notice in my worst moments, especially in my marriage, when it's gotten the most difficult is when I have lacked patience or a sense of humor in an important moment.

I don't want to become the class clown, but I think it's healthy to acknowledge my own foibles as well as those of others. For me, the idea is to be open to laughter. Whether I'm down on the ground among the shattered remains of a frail chair or waving a silly children's toy around in the dark in our backyard, it's about having some fun. It's a great gift to be able to laugh, especially at yourself. And the ability to laugh is a great way to relax others as well.

SECRETS TO REMEMBER

• Dogs don't take themselves too seriously. They have no dignity to uphold. That's what makes them so lovable.

• You should always have a sense of humor—especially about yourself. A little self-deprecating humor makes you much more human and interesting to family, friends, and coworkers.

• It's important to be able to laugh. Laughter is a great healer and a great release.

• The gift of laughter is always appreciated.

8 HAVING A GOAL (OR A PURPOSE) IS A GOOD THING

> "Many people fail in life, not for lack
> of ability or brains or even courage
> but simply because they have never
> organized their energies around a goal."
> — *Elbert Hubbard*

As he grew older, Exley had accumulated quite a reputation as a hunter. Unfortunately, though he was an excellent hunter, it was not as a bird dog. Too many days spent roaming the Brooklyn parks system turned him from what could easily have been an excellent career as a bird dog into a hunting machine.

As a German shorthair pointer, Exley's ancestors were bred by German sportsmen in the Victorian era as the über-hunting dog. He could hunt, point, flush, and retrieve, and he loved water. And Exley would have done them proud. But he wasn't great on point. He'd go on point for the count of three, maybe four, and then he'd start creeping toward his prey. This is an unforgivable sin in the pointing world. My father, Phil, hated that. He hated a gun dog who couldn't stand on point. "It's a waste of a good dog—it's a shame," he would say.

But my father and I were both in awe of Exley's gifts and determination. He had an unbelievable nose for rabbits, pheasants, squirrels, groundhogs—you name it. He could hunt by scent and sight. And he was magnificent in the field. He would hold his chocolate brown head above the bent autumn grass, scouring the field in a glance, his beige eyes alertly scanning the terrain for movement. In the next moment, his large, double-barreled nose twitched back and forth, scrubbing the air and earth for any clues or trails that led to his quarry.

THE GIFT OF THE FROZEN MIANUS

The first indication I had of Exley's incredible nose was on a January day in Connecticut. Exley always hated squirrels, and as hunters go, they would have easily classified him as "squirrelly," which has been the ruin of many a good gun dog. On this late-January day in Connecticut, we let Exley outside on my parents' property, where the ground was completely covered in ice and snow.

My parents, Anna and Eugenio, and I were having our

coffee and nibbling on coffee cake when there was a scratch at the door. The dogs—my parents' black mutt, Storm, and Exley—had been out for quite some time. My stepfather went to the door.

Anna and Eugenio are both great lovers of dogs. Eugenio is a thin, elegant man with a wicked sense of humor and a soft spot for anything furry. At one point, I discovered a drawer in my parents' kitchen when I was looking for a can opener. It was filled with cookies and candy bars. Eugenio saw me and told me to close it. "That's for the dogs," he said with a smile. He spoiled dogs rotten, and all dogs loved him. He paused in front of the door.

"Who is it?" he asked jokingly, and opened the door. Exley proudly trotted into the kitchen, head held high, little tail wagging, something in his mouth. "Carlo, get your dog. He's brought a stick into the house. You better get rid of it before your mother sees it." He bent down to retrieve the large stick from my dog's mouth, when he shot up with a start.

"Damn dog's brought in a frozen squirrel!" he said, shocked. "Come on, get this animal out of here!" he said, jerking his thumb over his shoulder. "Outside! Outside!"

My mother heard the commotion and was horrified. Exley returned later without a trophy and was allowed in, but he was shunned. Exley didn't help his situation when he later dug up a frozen fish from the cold, muddy banks of the Mianus River and dragged it into the house. He dropped it onto my mother's favorite Oriental carpet. Exley never let good manners get in the way of a successful day's hunt. Needless to say, the fish was not received warmly, and Exley found himself out on the frozen tundra again.

This story is only one of many such stories about his ability to sniff out prey and prizes in the world. This ability of his always amazed me and never failed to yield some kind of surprise.

THE SEAGULL

Exley was as happy in a swamp as he was in a pristine lake. And he loved the beach. The beaches in New Jersey are wonderful in spring, winter, and fall when dogs are permitted. You can walk your dog up and down the beach almost any time of day. Chelsea normally stayed as far from the water as possible, while Exley plunged right in. I liked to throw a tennis ball into the oncoming waves, and Exley dove in, headfirst, right through the wave. He came up on the other side, shaking his head, his ears flapping loudly, his brown head bobbing in the white sea foam. He paddled furiously to the ball, and then, grabbing it in his soft, bird dog's mouth, he returned to shore, riding the waves in like a born surfer. Once on shore, however, he dropped the ball, only momentarily, to shake himself off. While he was drying himself, Chelsea often stole the ball and proudly brought it to Dominique, as if she had done all the work.

One cold November day, Dominique and I decided to take the dogs to the beach. When we arrived, it was low tide, and the beach was flat, the cold sand dotted with little puddles. The day felt very romantic, and at one point, we were walking arm in arm as the dogs ran around on the deserted beach. And then we came upon a flock of seagulls.

Before I could even shout a command, Exley descended upon them.

Stealth was not on his mind as his paws pounded the wet, solidly packed sand. He raced down the beach, his paws slapping the wet sand, his collar jingling. As expected, the flock began to rise into the air as they realized that this thundering horde was none other than some lone, wacky dog, ears flapping, tongue hanging out.

Then the unthinkable happened. Exley leapt high up into the air, gracefully and beautifully, and in midair caught a huge seagull by the tail! He nabbed it like it was a Frisbee and brought it back down to earth. Our wintry romantic idyll was quickly shattered as we broke our loving gaze and arms and started racing down the beach, hollering at Exley.

He pranced around the beach, with this massive seagull sticking out of his mouth. Its large wings were flapping back and forth, and it was squawking loudly. With the massive bird in his mouth, all I could see was Exley's little tail bobbing back and forth.

Suddenly, there was a woman on the boardwalk, screaming at us. "Hey, what is your dog doing? Oh my god! Killer dog!! That dog is killing that poor bird! Help! Help!"

"Drop it! Drop it!" I yelled at Exley. Fortunately, he obeyed as soon as I got there, and he happily dropped the large, squawking, flapping bird. However, the seagull's tail sliced right into the soft wet sand so that it was stuck in the sand as surely as it had been stuck in Exley's mouth. Its wings were flapping, it was shrieking for its life, and its two little bird feet were sticking in the air, clawing, trying to get a hold of anything so it could right itself.

Of course, Exley thought it was the perfect time to go on point. He surely thought this was the second part of some exciting game. I was in the precarious position of trying to help the bird, who tried to peck at me anytime I came near it, while at the same time, I was holding off an excited 70-pound German shorthair pointer.

On the boardwalk, the lone woman had suddenly multiplied into a small group of people. I looked up as the sound of the catcalls increased. They were clamoring from the gray timbered railing. Shouts of "vicious animal," "attack dog," and "murderer!" rang through the air.

Chelsea, our shepherd, was barking back at them, and now Dominique had to go and subdue her. Finally, with Exley firmly in one hand, I got around behind the bird and nudged it forward. Its little feet finally gained traction, and the bird began waddling away.

Eyes bulging, Exley was horrified that I had helped the bird escape. He tried to lunge after it. I held him back, and Dominique and I both watched until the beleaguered fowl finally got its bearings and launched itself successfully into the air. We breathed a sigh of relief. We were glad to see that the bird appeared physically unharmed. But our relief was short-lived.

Now we turned, and suddenly, there was an angry mob. All manner of shouts were hurled at us as we attempted to race back to the car.

"Do you have a license for that animal?"

"Are you from around here? Where do you live?"

"That vicious animal should be destroyed!"

"You can't leave. We called the cops." The din did not sub-

side, and they followed us at a safe distance (they were afraid) and shouted obscenities at us as we scrambled into our little, dilapidated Subaru station wagon and putted off into the wintry sunset, our idyllic romantic adventure solidly behind us.

THE DEER STALKER

One wintry Sunday, Dominique and I were watching football when the first game of the day ended. The Giants were sched- uled to play the second game, starting at 4:00 p.m.

"Let's take the dogs for a walk over at the park," she said.

"Now?" I asked incredulously. "The Giants are coming on. I would have gone earlier, but not now." I was indignant.

"Well, I'm going," Dominique said in a huff. "These dogs need to get some exercise. And it wouldn't do you any harm either!"

"Dom, it's very late, and it's getting dark outside. Seriously, I don't think it's a good idea."

"And I don't think it's a good idea to sit in the house all day watching football!" I heard the jingle-jangle of the leashes and collars, and she, Exley, and Chelsea were gone.

I felt bad after the station wagon pulled away. She was

taking them to a very large park, and she was right. The dogs (and maybe I) needed to get outside. Especially Exley. I had not been as diligent about walking Exley in the suburbs as I had been in New York. The idea of getting in our other car and sur- prising her at the park popped into my mind. Imagine how many points I could score doing something like that. But this silly urge quickly passed once I resettled into the couch with a new, cold beer in hand and the game beginning.

Around halftime, as I was beginning to worry about not having caught up with her, Dom came running in, sobbing. She was fighting to catch her breath.

"I lost Exley."

"You're kidding me, right?" I asked, alarmed.

"I lost him. There were some deer running through the woods, and he took off after them. I called him and called him, and he didn't come back. I chased him, but he didn't come."

"Didn't you go looking for him?"

"Of course! But I couldn't find him."

"How could you lose the dog? You lost the dog?"

I was off the couch in a shot and was dressed in seconds, barking out a string of directions and expletives. Dominique, a much more responsible and responsive dog owner than I ever was, was both scared and embarrassed.

We took separate cars. The park was officially closed, but I didn't care and raced around the barriers and through a stand of trees to get in. I drove quickly through the park, windows down, calling out his name. It grew dark outside, and with the high beams on, I passed sleeping deer, foraging deer, and all other forms of forest wildlife, all the while screaming out Exley's name.

At one point, I went up a country lane to a house and small farm that someone had pointed me toward, saying they had seen a dog run that way. I walked up the drive and was met by two men. They were dressed in black pressed pants and alligator shoes and wore black overcoats and sunglasses. They spoke with heavy, laden voices. And in the driveway, there were a dozen cars. But the house was quiet. Only a few lights were on. This was an increasingly odd scenario to encounter as I searched frantically for Exley.

"Where you goin'?" I was asked.

"Hi! I'm looking for my dog. Someone said my dog raced up this driveway."

They both shook their heads no. "I'm sorry, my friend. You gotta go."

"Yeah, but I'm looking for my dog. I see you have some fields over there." I cupped my hands around my mouth. "EXLEY!!!!!"

"Yo, whadda you doin', man? I said there ain't no dog. And you can't be yellin' like that. You gotta leave."

Some verbal sparring ensued. I left perplexed, but peaceably. They certainly weren't farmers.

About 5 minutes later, I got in the car and did a lap around the outside of the park, wandering the back roads, looking for my dog. I was so worried. Then I came around one corner, and on the street was a stopped car. The driver was standing by his car with a dog. It was Exley!

The couple had been driving when Exley suddenly shot out of nowhere in front of them. They had hit him, accidentally, and broken the headlight of their car.

"I think he's okay," the man said. He was nicely dressed, in a fine black leather jacket and black Italian loafers. He smelled of aftershave and wore an expensive watch.

Conversely, I was in sweatpants and a Giants baseball hat, and Exley was covered in mud and smelled like deer. It was awful. I explained what had happened, and I thanked the man, offering to pay for the headlight. I gave him my phone number, but he never called.

We got Exley home, gave him a warm bath and some hot broth, and he slept fine. The next morning, he moved a little stiffly, but was fine. Months later, we found out that the small, secluded farmhouse in our idyllic little town had been bought by mobsters and was being used as a bordello. The police raided it and closed it down. I knew those two weren't farmers.

THE NIGHT VISITOR

In the middle of one summer night, I was awoken by a blood-curdling scream. My wife screamed like there was a man at the end of our bed with a knife the size of a machete. It was pitch-black, and she continued to scream with the covers pulled over her head. Without my glasses on, I squinted hard as I quickly scanned the room.

"What! What is it? Who is it?"

"Bat! Bat! It's a bat!!" she cried. Dominique had been as dead asleep as I was. But she had been awakened by Exley jumping up and down as high as he possibly could. She told him to lie down. When he wouldn't listen, she opened her eyes, only to find a bat circling the room. He was jumping up and down trying to catch the bat!

We were now both covering our heads, and my wife was still screaming. My wife, Dominique, the woman who was raised on a farm and who extolled me with her many brave feats of an-imal daring, was now cowering under the sheets.

"Where's Chelsea?" I asked.

"She's under the bed!" We decided to make a run for it. Dom, the big white German shepherd, and I scampered out of the room while Exley completely ignored us, jumping and lunging at the intruder.

With baseball hats on and weapons in hand, we reentered the room. Dom had a broom, and I had a mop. We opened a window, hoping in vain to coerce the unwanted and probably frightened visitor away.

The bat suddenly leapt from its safe hiding place and began circling the room. As it fluttered past us, we both swung at it, trying to strike it down. Dominique swung, and the bat dipped low to avoid her broom. Exley leapt in midair and proudly brought it down. He shook it hard. As usual, he drew no blood. He shook it violently to its death, dropped it, and waited for it to move again. He was sadly disappointed.

He was happily surprised the next day, when Dominique made him a steak dinner. Exley never had a prouder moment. He had reasserted his role as house protector and firmly established himself in my wife's eyes as guardian extraordinaire.

EVERYONE NEEDS A JOB

Almost every breed of dog was developed or adapted by man for a specific job. And dogs love their jobs. Dalmatians were bred to run alongside coaches and to guard the horses. Bernese mountain dogs were bred as cart animals. Pointers, setters, beagles, and foxhounds were bred to hunt. Many terriers were bred as ratters. Shepherds, sheepdogs, Malanois, and collies were bred for herding. Dogs love jobs. Jobs give purpose and meaning to dogs' lives. The happiest dogs I know are the ones allowed to do their jobs in some fashion.

If your whole life's ambition was to fetch, because it's what generations of genealogy had bred you to do, and no one ever threw a ball for you, never got you to run, never made you dive into the water after a stick or ball, but instead kept you cooped up in a house all day with only a quick in or out for bathroom pit stops, do you think you'd be happy? I know I would probably be gritting my teeth. I'd need to really rip into something—something worthy of all my pent-up aggression. A plastic bone wouldn't get it done for me. A real bone might not do it for me, and some people don't understand that. And that's where their problems begin.

Do you know one human being that doesn't want to be valued? Are dogs and people so different? I know a lot of elderly people who are young because they are active and useful in their golden years. Conversely, I know a lot of younger adults who are old because they have lost their way and seem to have no goal, no sense of being involved or being needed.

Exley's exploits were well known and valued. One couple wanted us to leave him in Maine with them for a week or two so he could clear their backyard of squirrels. My neighbor borrowed Exley one time when a bat came into his house. I must admit, I gushed some pride as I saw my neighbor's silhouette move across his lace-curtained window, complete with baseball bat, tennis racket, and Exley's stubby tail trailing across the large window's expanse. When Exley came home from my neighbor's house, he acted like an excited little kid.

Exley was never so proud as when he had flushed game or caught an intruder. His head held high, his gait bouncy, his chest held out, his little tail wagging. A little pride in life goes a long way, especially after being acknowledged.

A PURPOSE OR A GOAL

During his lifetime, Exley caught six squirrels, two groundhogs, a robin, a duck, a bat, and a seagull, as well as many of those elusive gazelle-type creatures known as garbage cans. Hunting gave Exley a reason to get up in the morning. It gave purpose to his life.

Exley fought age every step of the way. Like most middle-aged men, he attempted often to perform the feats his younger body had so easily accomplished. Some of these ill-conceived attempts landed him in the vet's office. Eventually, Exley started to slow down. We both did. The years and the mileage were catching up with us. Our walks didn't last quite as long. Exley didn't run quite as fast, nor did he wander quite as far. Every so often, in the middle of hunting, he looked up to check my whereabouts. He got up a little slower, and it took him a little longer to get up the stairs or into the back of the station wagon. And after a good day's hunt, he slept a little later and got up a little stiffer. But the fire in his eyes never died. Not ever. They were always bright and alert.

Maybe dogs are the lucky ones. Because they are bred for specific tasks, there's not much doubt about what they should be doing—about what they like to do. But for a lot of us people, figuring out what makes us happy is a big part of the problem. As I played ball with Exley and walked with him in the woods, I tried to think about my life and career. I tried to focus on my family and my work—and my goals for each—that were essential to me.

Have you ever seen a bored dog? They get very antsy. They get anxious. They begin to behave badly. When dogs are not directed, exercised, or worked, they get bored and destructive. I have found I am the same way. If I lose focus on my life, I find, looking back sometimes, that I have gotten sidetracked in bad or destructive behavior. In that respect, I think people and dogs are much the same.

There are so many distractions in life. Exley's single-mindedness was an inspiration. If I could only focus like he did, maybe I would be as efficient and happy as he was. Exley was always working. I admired that in him. Whether he was being a watchdog guarding our house or a hunter in the field, Exley valued his role in our lives. In retrospect, I realize that it was one of the traits I admired in him most. And I realize that doing these things made him happy. And I realize in this way we were much more alike than I wanted to admit.

But this lesson would soon be lost on me, for his greatest lessons were about to be realized, and I didn't even know it.

- Dogs need a goal. Whether it's just keeping you company or guarding your house, yard, and family, or more specific work or activities, dogs love, nay need, to be needed.

- Like dogs, people want a job. Just like dogs, people want to be needed.

- Sometimes the way to make yourself valuable to others is by volunteering or participating in community, church, or other civic activism. The involvement will make you a happier person, and more people will want to be around you.

9 ADULTHOOD

"Twenty years a child; 20 years running wild;
20 years a mature man—and after that, praying."

—Irish proverb

This penultimate lesson that Exley taught me, this lasting gift, was so subtle that I did not understand for some time. But in fact, it may have been the most important one. I find that most people, especially men, are averse to this lesson and look to put off the value of such a lesson for as long as possible. Adulthood means commitment, which in turn means loss as far as most single men are concerned. However, it was Exley who taught me that love, devotion, responsibility, and routine all had their own rewards. To the single man, these are dirty words—and to some women I have known too. But I did not realize the power of these words; I did not realize the power of adulthood until I was knee deep in it. And it is a beautiful thing.

EMPTY ARMS

By the year 2000, Dominique and I had been battling infertility for almost 6 years. It had taken a toll on us both mentally and emotionally. Dealing with infertility is a little like going through Elisabeth Kübler-Ross's five stages of grief. We had struggled through anger, denial, and the other emotions. Because, in essence, it is a small death you feel inside of you that is difficult to explain to those people who have not been dealt this blow.

We had gritted our way through one round of in vitro fertilization. The ups and downs of that process were unbearable. The injections. The highs and lows due to the drugs. The highs and lows of hopes and dreams. At one point, right after the eggs were implanted, the doctors gave us a photograph of the two eggs, taken with a microscope. Dominique clutched the photograph for dear life and carried it with her from that first day, a mixture of hope and desperation. Ten days later, when the in vitro failed and our growing hopes shattered, she was devastated. We accepted our fate. With in vitro, you have a 50 percent chance of success the first time, a 25 percent chance the second time, and your odds don't improve after that. We knew some people who'd done it three, four, five times. The whole experience had been disappointing, and for a while, we considered a child-free existence, with just the two of us, and Exley and Chelsea.

Especially through this period, the dogs were a source of consolation and sympathy. There is something, is seems to me, that dogs instantly understand. They are excellent judges of mood. And during this period, they were very affectionate and solicitous. Not in their usual way. During moments when either of us was feeling down, one of the dogs would come gently to us and cuddle next to us. Exley, a broad-chested, strong, and willful animal at times, easily slid onto the couch next to me and calmly molded himself against me and snuggled in, his big, soft, chocolate brown head nestling in next to my chin. It was as though they understood. There were a lot of days we spent looking out the windows, wondering what we were to do with the rest of our lives.

At one point, Dominique wanted to bury the photograph in the back of the yard, but she was afraid Exley would dig it up. I too was worried. She was not deterred, though, and indeed buried the photograph in the backyard, burying with it our hopes of bearing our own children. It was symbolic while at the same time very real. And I am happy to say that Exley did not, in fact, dig it up, much to my own amazement.

We poured our energy back into the dogs. And as always, it paid off. We went for walks in the park, and Dominique worked with Exley on agility and Chelsea too. And as the year passed, we began to look into adoption. Like many, we went to adoption conferences and looked into foreign adoption. Children were available from everywhere on the globe. China, Korea, South America, Central America, Vietnam, Russia, Eastern Europe. At one point, there was a strange confluence of events, and my wife and I were turned toward Waiting Children. We had decided to adopt older children, somewhere between 3 and 10 years old. These children, like in vitro fertilization, had inverse ratios of successful adoption. The older a child gets, the more unlikely it is that he or she will be adopted. And there are thousands of perfectly good children who slowly go through a system of foster homes and group homes before they find themselves 18 years old, freed from the government's benign neglect, and sent out into the world alone. I can only think that the people who help most of these unclaimed children are in fact saints or angels, regardless of their own personal foibles.

In 2001, we began registering with agencies and checking out Web sites. We took a course and went through fostering and adoption classes sponsored by the state. At the same time, a house we had coveted for some time also became available, and so we moved, one block down the same street. Exley and Chelsea loved it. The house was bigger, and the yard was bigger. Not only was the yard bigger, but it was also poorly fenced in. Exley soon discovered a way out of the yard and became a roving gadabout. It was a few weeks before I discovered where he was sneaking out, but by then he had developed a little routine of roaming the neighborhood, making stops with those people who routinely gave him treats, or who inadvertently had left him some tasty morsels in their unguarded or unprotected garbage cans. He was quite popular. With his Marmaduke-like gait, he amiably bobbed up and down the little streets, happily greeting those he passed. He barked at back doors and knocked over garbage cans with regularity, I found out much later. He had to be stopped. I got a piece of new fencing and placed the large panel in front of the offending hole. But Ex was strong, and he literally knocked the fence over and completed his self-appointed rounds. I eventually won the battle, but not before Exley had probed and found several more weak spots in the old wooden fence.

By this time, Exley's face was starting to change. Middle-age had ringed his nose with white; the deep chocolate brown head of his youth was ghostly in its pallor. Exley, now 11, was getting old. When we went upstairs at night, he still waited for me halfway up the stairs, his front paws on one step and hindquarters on another, just waiting for me to ascend. I would climb the stairs, happy to see my old friend. "Hey there, old man, what's up," I would say. He would bow his head and nuzzle me as I drew near, and the two of us would greet each other thusly almost every night. He would then turn and follow me when I finally gained the top of the stairs, after our ritual greeting was completed, and take his place on the dog bed in our room. Chelsea would wait at the top of the stairs, her big white head and pink nose greeting me, supplicant but loving.

In February of 2002, after several false starts, we were notified of two little boys in Iowa who needed a home. Their mother had decided to give them up for adoption because she was unable to care for them. We jumped on a plane and flew out to Council Bluffs. We were both as apprehensive as could be and were not sure what to expect. The boys were fraternal twins, and $3\frac{1}{2}$ years old. We had traded pictures via the agency facilitating the adoption, and so we knew what they looked like and vice versa, and of course, they also had pictures of the dogs.

When we first saw Dylan and Dawson, we literally held our collective breaths. We had been worried that we might not react well or might blanch when confronted for the first time. What if we didn't like them? What if they didn't like us? However, like with Exley, we both could not believe our eyes, nor they theirs. It was love at first sight. They were beautiful little boys, smart, alert, and cheerful. The mother was deathly sad to give the boys up, but realized that she could not provide them with a stable, loving home. The boys had lived with a string of relatives, often apart from their mother. But it was obvious that she was devastated by the situation. We had several long talks with her over the ensuing weeks, and then she called us and told us she had made up her mind: She wanted the boys to live with us. In retrospect, it was the bravest thing I have ever known someone to do. She could not provide them the attention, the security, and the background that we could and loved her children enough to want them to have better than she could provide. In the intervening years, we have grown to have a great respect for her, and she us. We talk often.

THE GREATEST MONSTER KILLER IN NEW JERSEY

Suffice it to say, the new house was now about to be readied for two new princes. And they were both keen on meeting Exley and Chelsea. They were excited about having their own dogs. They were both convinced Exley was a Dalmatian, and it was hard to get them to understand that Ex was a German shorthair, not a Dalmatian. But they loved him anyway.

From the day they arrived, Exley was an instant favorite. Chelsea, always skittish near children, did her best to avoid them, these two miniature invaders. But Exley, ever the sponge of all affection, was happy to accept their attention. Whether they hugged him too hard, hit him, slapped him, fell over him, as children that age are wont to do, he happily suffered their presence and followed them around to no end. He had always been an excellent watchdog; his role was now even more important, and it seemed he cherished the role, because he played it to the hilt. He'd sit on the porch, or in the backyard, and watch over the two little yahoos wreaking havoc, and bark at any passerby.

Dylan and Dawson were amazed at Exley, and no more so than at bedtime. As young children often are, they were afraid of the dark. Especially 1,500 miles from the only series of places they had ever known as home. The first few weeks, it was difficult for them to go to sleep. We bought a television and video player, and let them fall asleep watching some children's movie, but invariably talk of monsters entered into the conversation, and thus was Exley's greatest job ever assigned.

Sleep should come easy to them, we said, because, of course, Exley, to their great pleasure, began sleeping in the boys' room. And he was, of course, the world's greatest monster killer. Not only had he slain squirrels and groundhogs and bats! But he was one of the most decorated monster killers in the history of killing monsters. The boys at first were skeptical and demanded

I provide several of his adventures as proof. I recounted many such tales for them before they finally came to believe.

Our nightly forays were slightly changed. Exley still waited for me at the top of the stairs, but his wizened face drooped a little more. And together, we would saunter into the boys' room. Sometimes, he was already up there with Dom and the boys and would happily greet me, as would Chelsea. But in the end, he would lie down in their room and sleep. Every night, we would go into the room, after the boys were asleep, and tuck them in. Then Exley would leave the room and follow us into ours.

He would curl up in his bed, and I would get down on my knees and, kneeling over, I would pet him. "Hey, old man," I would say. "Did you take care of my boys tonight? You're a good man. You better not go anywhere," I used to tease him. "They have a lot of growing up to do. You have to help me raise these two boys. You better take care of yourself." I think back on these moments, which we oft repeated, and I still wonder why I said those things. "Hey, old man, you better not go anywhere." I realize that as excited as I was about the boys' arrival—and I was ecstatic—I knew Exley was getting old too. He was $9\frac{1}{2}$ years old now, and his face was gray with age. Exley was no Dorian Gray; each year on, his face was ringed with yet a little more white. His expressive eyes were now circled with hoary age. Only the top of his head remained the deep cocoa color.

But for a while, we lived an idyllic life I will never forget. I remember sitting in the barn of the new house, where I had made an office out of two old horse stalls, me and my computer and some old, ratty furniture, and I would hear the kids laughing, running around the yard, and my wife speaking and the dogs barking, and I would think to myself that I had died and gone to heaven. For all the pain and anguish we had suffered over the childless years, it seemed God, or whatever great power was out there, luck, somewhere, had led me to heaven. And it seemed too good to be true, to be able to experience this great moment in life with my wife and our dogs, especially Exley, my friend.

It was fall, and I had come home, and Dominique told me that Exley had hurt himself. It seemed he had torn his knee apart again. A series of visits to the vet confirmed that he had torn his knee, and it was not worth repairing at this age. Even if we were to repair the knee, as we had done 5 years earlier, his hip was so devastated by arthritis that he would never put any substantial weight on it again anyway. Exley hobbled through Christmas and the harsh, cold winter. Sometimes he howled in pain, and I knew it hurt him, because he never howled—not when he broke his leg, not when he desocked himself, not when he was hit by a car the second time. But now he let out a gut-tural howl that came from his gut.

We went to two vets, both of whom gave us anti-inflammatories and painkillers. And it seemed, at times, that he was getting better. But he would push himself. He was not as thunderously fast as he had been in his youth, when he brazenly leapt over retired racing greyhounds or rammed into other unsuspecting dogs. He could not turn on an instant, and his reflexes were slow. Exley did not age gracefully, for he could not accept that his body could not live up to the standards he demanded of it. And so, when he tried to leap three steps and failed, when he cut too quickly on the wrong leg, when he tried to press against Chelsea while they wrestled, like he had in the old days, he would collapse and howl.

And when the moment passed, and he was himself again, I would kneel down and comfort him, saying, "Hey, old man, you think you're scaring me. You're not scaring me. You're not going anywhere. You're staying right here. Yes, you are, and you're going to help me raise these two boys. You aren't going anywhere." And then I'd offer him a cookie, which always perked his spirits right up. But I was lying to myself and to him. It is even hard to admit that now. A friend was over one day when Exley let out a howl, and he said he thought it was more serious. But being used to his arthritis by now, I dismissed it. I look back on that moment as sheer and utter denial on my part and curse myself, even now.

THE DOG MAKES THE MAN

On May 10 and 11, 2003, it was a great weekend. And Exley seemed to be getting better. His leg did not bother him a lot, and he moved fairly gracefully. It was warm and sunny, and the boys played outside, and we grilled on the deck and ate outside in the warm sun. Chelsea and Exley wrestled nicely, and Dominique and I were encouraged. It seemed winter was over, and maybe with the warmer weather, Exley's arthritis might not pose such a problem.

But the next morning, coming down the stairs, I saw that the front hall carpet was stained with a huge brown spot. Exley had soiled a carpet for maybe only the third time in his life with me. One had been in his drunken binge, and the other had been when I refused to let him out when he was truly sick (and I didn't know, but he had let me know), which I considered my own fault. In this instance, I cursed him, but not too badly, for he had done something like this so infrequently. When my wife came home that afternoon, he had done it again. And the next morning, it happened again. I looked at the floor and then at him. His eyes were sad and ashamed, and I felt then a pang of worry, of fear. We knew something was wrong. He would not eat his breakfast, and we immediately made plans to bring him to the vet. We both assumed he must have eaten something in one of his neighborhood forays that had finally caught up with him. There had been more than one time when I had to pull a plastic bag or a piece of rope dangling from his hindquarters, the telltale sign of his most grotesque binges. Dominique packed Ex into the station wagon. We had determined that she would drop him off before going to work and would bring him home either at lunch or at the end of the day.

I will never forget it as long as I live. I was in a taxicab with my boss and friend, Buz Teacher, on the way to The Palm for a meeting with the design director and associate director of our company, when Dominique called me. She was crying, and I couldn't understand her. At first, I thought she was upset about one of the boys. But I realized she was talking about my friend.

Exley had cancer. He was dying. The cancer had eaten away his intestines, and there was nothing they could do for him. I had to come home right away. They wanted to put him down. And I told Dom that no one was to touch him until I got there—no one. I hung up the phone, tears streaming down my face. I excused myself as I openly sobbed. Buz was as nice as he could have possibly been. I took a cab back to the office and raced home. Speeding all the way back to Jersey, I could barely see, as tears welled up in my eyes. What had I done to him? What had I done to my friend?

The hospital scene was awful. Suffice it to say that they had rehydrated the poor animal, who was slowly drowning within his own skin with every thirsty sip of water he lapped up. Between the intravenous fluids and several bowlfuls of water, Exley was looking better than he had that morning. But the tube attached to his right forepaw was there for one thing, and as soon as I made it into the room, I knew what was going to happen.

Dominique was a mess. Crying. Wailing. And Exley, who had always hated the vet's office, paced uncontrollably. I lay down on the floor in my suit, and I clutched him as I never had before. I am sure I must have scared him silly. The doctors explained that we really had no choice. There was no one on call who could put him down if we took him back home, and two doctors assured us he wouldn't make the night.

But I sat there on the floor for hours. I couldn't do it to my friend. I couldn't do it. This animal I had spent the better part of 10 years, most of my adult life, nursing, and feeding, and nurturing, I could not do this to my friend. It went against every fiber of my being. This was the companion who had seen me through incredible personal lows and wonderful, glowing highs. This vessel I had poured every part of myself into. I fought the decision as long as I could, hugging him and cuddling him.

Eventually, reality set in, and so did the coming of the night. Approving that ugly moment is the single worst thing I have ever had to do. I cried and cried and closed my eyes when the doctor hooked the needle up to the tube. I gritted my teeth. I kissed him and said, "I'm going to see you again, old man. I'm not done with you yet. I love you, Exley. I love you. I will always love you. I'm going to see you again. Yes, I will." He closed his eyes, and then I felt his body go limp, and I heard a sigh come out of his mouth. He was gone, and I let out a wail as deep and as sad and as guttural as those when he cried out in pain, and I hated myself.

Dominique and I drove home, me following her. We then went and picked up the boys and took them for pizza. We tried to explain over dinner what had happened in the cheeriest way possible, and the boys seemed to accept the news we had given them without much pause. They were more concerned with who got pepperoni and who got root beer. And Dominique and I looked at each other and shrugged. But when it came time to go to bed, Dawson and Dylan were beside themselves. Especially Dawson. Where was Exley? Why wasn't he here?

Why wasn't he coming back? Tears started. Theirs. Mine. Ours.

I lay in bed that night, talking to myself, long after Dominique fell asleep. And I talked to Exley too. I tried to explain how sorry I was for any time I might have taken him for granted or not loved him enough. I wanted to tell him how sorry I was. And I wanted to tell him how angry I was for his leaving, leaving me — and the boys. I said to me, "You were supposed to be here and help me raise those boys."

I was a 40-year-old man with a family and an important job. I was no longer the 29-year-old wisecracking associate editor. I was now a publisher. I was someone people looked to for direction, and here I was, babbling to myself, my eyes welling up.

But it occurred to me over the subsequent days that it was not Exley's job to raise those boys; it was my job, as I had known all along. It had been Exley's job to raise me. All that time, we had been having fun, going for walks, getting into trouble, being companions and friends in some great adventure. And I had spent so much time teaching him: sit, stay, down, roll over. But all along, he had been teaching me: responsibility, devotion, routine, commitment. And I realized that was one of the greatest secrets that damn dog ever taught me. It is the child that makes the man, and in this case, it was a dog. All along, it had been the dog doing the teaching, not me. How do you like that?

The funny thing is—it doesn't matter if it's a thing, a pet, or another human being (although I happen to think loving a pet or another human being is more rewarding, because they can love you back). Commitment and routine sound like deadly words—serious and boring. But when they happen to involve someone you love, someone you look forward to seeing and you deeply care about, then those words are inseparable.

And responsibility is one of those nasty words your parents tried to teach you. It was almost a four-letter word when I was a kid, my parents tried to ground it into me so hard. But with Exley, I would not have had it any other way. I didn't want anyone but me to be responsible for him. His safety, his well-being, his happiness were my responsibility, and it was one of the great gifts in my life to have been responsible for him. Missing drinks out with my friends. Getting up early on Saturdays and Sundays and walking him in the park, feeding him, no matter how well I felt—these were not real hardships. I was more than happy to choose him every time for 10 years. The hardest part of letting go was that I had enjoyed the responsibility and taken such great pride in my ability to keep him happy and well fed and healthy for those years. Despite everything I have accomplished in life, I took greater pride in his longevity and well-being than anything else I have ever done.

This has also helped me in business, because I think it makes me a better person as a worker and as a supervisor. It makes me understand that I need to be more mindful of the person above me. I need to fit into their plan for the group in which I am working. And it makes me more mindful of the people who work for me. These lessons have taught me to be more attentive to their needs and more mindful of their future than I might have been in the past.

Today I am the responsible one. I am the one who says, "No, you cannot come to work in cutoffs and flip-flops on casual Friday." I have to lay down rules like "No headphones while you're working at your desk." I am the one who has to remind editors to fill out forms and file for checks and who stands in the way of their most important acquisitions. I harass them about catalog and flap copy. I try to help them in their young careers. Sometimes they listen; sometimes they don't. I try to have patience.

When I was in the later stages of my career at Running Press, the executives all had to go to New York. It was summer, and while we were stuck in meetings in New York, some of the younger staff members had a cookout. They brought in beer, a grill, hot dogs, hamburgers, and a boom box and had themselves a grand old time in the back cement courtyard of our building. I feigned chagrin. Fire codes, insurance, safety, blah, blah, blah. Secretly, I envied their soirée and felt pissed because I hadn't thought of it myself. Still, most of them looked at me, then in my early forties, and couldn't imagine my youth at all.

Exley was not a saint by any measure. He was a clown, and a hardhead, and a great friend. And I am not a saint. I may not have been the best owner in the world. Maybe I was selfish at times, and maybe I was forgetful others. I don't deny any of that. And indeed, I wince some days when I am in the shower and remember suddenly some thoughtless transgression I may have done against my friend. Maybe I stayed out later than I meant to, maybe I forgot to give him medicine, or maybe I hollered at him when I shouldn't have. I wince with embarrassment and shame. I ask him for forgiveness, and I ask it of you. But I am also very proud. I understand that my boys' needs and wants are more important than mine. I have more patience for them (despite my wife's sometime denial of that quality) than I would have if it had not been for Exley. I may not be the best dad in the world. I am very human, and I am very fallible. But I have more of the qualities I need to and have a better understanding than I might have had he not been there for me.

And I think I am a better husband. Again, I may sometimes be thoughtless or forgetful. I may seem too quiet sometimes, too loud others. But I believe the faith, love, and devotion I have given to my wife are what I understand are the meanings of a contract between two living beings because I learned them from Exley. As I said earlier, that dog was one damn fine teacher.

SECRETS TO REMEMBER

- Taking care of a pet, especially a dog, teaches us about commitment, routine, and responsibility (these are not four-letter words).

- Commitment, routine, and responsibility are not weights that weigh us down but are rather an implicit contract that we keep with ourselves and another (that we would not have any other way).

- Maturity is not something you reach on your own. It comes by way of others. It comes through responsibility and trust.

- Caring for another life is one of the most awesome responsibilities that nature has to offer. Embracing such a contract is one of the great joys of life.

10 A TRUE FRIEND IS A FRIEND FOR LIFE

"The glory of friendship is not the outstretched hand, nor the kindly smile . . . it's the spiritual inspiration that comes to one when he discovers that someone else believes in him and is willing to trust him with his friendship."
— *Ralph Waldo Emerson*

There is a lot to remember Exley by. We have many family photos together. We have the books wherein I, or others, wrote about him. We even have videotape. And I cannot lie. Over the intervening period, from time to time, I have watched one in particular. It is not what you would think it to be. But it was something worthwhile to me.

It was his last Christmas with us, with me. We had just gotten the video camera, and I was taping the boys' first Christmas with us. I had wanted to capture their every move from the morning of Christmas Eve to nightfall of Christmas day. They made Christmas so much fun. Their constant excitement. Their wonderment. Their joy and youthful mischievousness. All of it was infectious.

The videotape is of our holiday, filled with relatives, scampering dogs, running children, and presents. Across the screen, the two boys scamper, clad in footsie pajamas, dogs trailing, mother and father now shouting, now laughing. Relatives chatting.

But like the many ironies in life, while the videotape celebrates this first, exciting Christmas, it also commemorates a very special and last moment with my friend of 10 years. I had no idea then. Old as he was, I truly thought we would celebrate one or two more holidays together.

The videotape shows me and my family with all our warts — ah, well, I never said I, or we, were perfect. Like all home movies, I suspect, this one has lots of wasted footage. I span the house Christmas Eve, dotted by the tumbleweeds of crumpled balls of wrapping paper and bows. The dining room table littered with half-filled glasses, a few lingering used dessert dishes, and an odd assortment of wrappers from chocolates and mints. And then I pan into the kitchen, where my wife is washing the dishes. She sees me, rightly curses me, and tells me to put down the camera and help out by doing something.

The next morning's taping went well, filled with squeals of joy and torrents of laughter as the boys voraciously ripped apart the papers and bows that held the secrets of Santa's bounty. Toys of all shapes and sizes. Fire engines. Hot Wheels. Play-Doh. Videos. Books. Candy. And, yes, there were a few grumbles (for any box containing clothes).

My parents Phil and Joanne arrived first. And Phil, with his booming voice and giant face, greeted Exley with a big hello. "Hey there, old fella! Merry Christmas, you old son of a gun. Come here!" he said, his arms welcoming Exley like an old friend. Exley greeted my father enthusiastically, if a little stiffly. Phil petted him, rubbing him just behind his big, floppy ears. I felt great pride in watching my father greet Exley so enthusiastically. I felt a father's pride—the same as watching a grandfather greeting his grandson, or two old men embracing each other.

Then came the relatives and views of the newly set table, with its shining silver appointments and sparkling crystal glasses. The commensurate oohs and aahs. And of course, more peals of laughter and excitement as we entered another round of presents and their attendant cheers. The dogs brushing against the Christmas tree. The gorging on festive foods and sinful desserts. And lots of wine and port. And there is a shot of Exley and Chelsea sharing the roasting pan, chomping at scraps, and savoring the drippings to the very last.

At the end of the evening, I posted the camera on a tripod and recorded our conversations as we settled into the living room. The boys were in bed now. And it was my parents and aunt, my sister Leigh, and my wife. We settled in with the fireplace ablaze with a dozen candles, and my wife snuggled into a blanket in the living room of our Victorian house. It was quite the scene.

I happened to take the only open chair, a large crème-colored wingback chair, which was nearest the camera. You could not see me, because my head kept leaning back, behind the wing of the backrest. Exley had been pacing through the room, which had now grown increasingly smaller with everyone in it and all the presents strewn about. Dominique kept telling him to go lie down. The room was small, and she was not wrong. But Exley kept circling around, and eventually, he came to me. And he sat himself down and nudged my hand with his nose, and I began to pet him.

And to me, as strange as this may sound, with my two sons sleeping upstairs, this was my favorite moment of the entire 2 days. My family around me, the Christmas tree twinkling with light, the kids asleep upstairs (exhausted from opening too many presents), the fireplace giving off a warm glow, and my best friend sitting right beside me. I petted him slowly and calmly, talking to everyone else in the room, petting that dog the entire time.

At one point, I looked down at him and said, "Exley, you are the best present I ever got." And I meant it. He was my friend and confidant. He was my salve and my pride. And there was no Christmas in my life while he was alive that I did not cherish completely his company and his being. And I just kept petting him and petting him until the tape ran out.

President George Washington once wrote, "Friendship is a plant of slow growth and must undergo and withstand the shocks of adversity before it is entitled to the appellation." There was a time when I could not have understood his quote. I understand it now. But the trials and tribulations of our life-time together, the good and the bad, are happy memories now.

My Christmas memory of Exley is an appropriate and good memory, for holidays are when he is missed most and where we talk of him often. In the subsequent seasons, whether in spring, summer, or fall, whenever we gather together with friends or family, someone never fails to bring him up, and a story is remembered, and we begin to laugh and wonder where the time has gone.

CHELSEA WAS A FRIEND TOO

Chelsea too was thrown for a loss. Weeks passed, and she sat at the door again, as she had when she first came to us, and looked

out the door, seemingly looking for her missing friend. Whenever the door to the house opened or closed, she always greeted the entrant enthusiastically, and then ran to the door and looked to see if anyone else was here (something she had not done before). And whenever she passed the cars, she began stopping and jumping up to see if he might be in one of them (again, something new). Eventually she tired of this, but there was no mistaking the melancholy in her face and demeanor.

THE CANINE CAN OPENER

So maybe the best story about friendship, though, in the end, doesn't belong to me and my friend, but to Exley and Chelsea. One holiday, while we were in our first house in New Jersey, we were on the holiday house tour. We had worked very hard to clean the house, paint it, refurbish it, and find the right mixture of antiques and knickknacks to create a traditional, if not Victorian, feel. The house was festooned with garlands and a kissing ball and a tree decorated with old antique ornaments from the 1940s that we'd bought for $5 for a whole box at a tag sale somewhere in the town. The entire house was overrun with poinsettias and wreaths and bows.

I had even gone to the town's hall of records and the Monmouth County Historical Society and found out about the past owners of the house. In more than 100 years, no more than four families had lived in the home.

For the tour, we bought a big punch bowl and three or four extremely large tins of Danish butter cookies, for the more than 600 to 700 people who took the house tour that day. The dogs were locked out back on the porch or fenced in with baby gates penned in the kitchen. Many people came and petted the dogs. Some snuck them a cookie. Everyone had some punch and some cookies. It was a lovely and fun day.

However, we did have an unopened tin of cookies left. The seal was still tight around the tin lid, taping the can closed tightly. The tin sat first on the kitchen table, then the counter, and finally on a shelf in the pantry.

One Saturday a month or two later, we went out for the day, and we left the pantry door open by mistake. Of course, it was our own fault. When we returned, many hours later, the dogs were asleep on the couch, too tired to move when we came home. And on the floor was the blue tin. The lid to the tin was still sealed on tightly, but the top of the tin was ripped open from the center. It looked as if an alien had burst forth from inside the tin. Little sections peeled back. The shiny, clean metal interior

was still sparkly inside, with nary a cookie to be found. The tape had held. But the metal of the lid couldn't keep them at bay.

Littered all over the house were the little cupcake-like paper holders that had held the cookies in place. We found them in the kitchen, in the den, in the living room, in the dining room, on the stairs, and on the landing of the second floor. At first we were angry, but then Dominique started to giggle.

"What the heck are you laughing at?"

"I was thinking how cute they must have looked from behind, pulling the cookies out and their tails wagging. They must have been so happy."

And it was probably true. The view must have been hilarious. Exley's little tail wagging. Chelsea's big, furry tail going back and forth. And the happy gorging that must have gone on. We both laughed.

For months and months, and even later when we moved, we were continually finding those little crimped, cupcake-like paper holders everywhere. Behind the sofa. Under the chest. Under the sideboard in the dining room. Long after we had put the incident behind us, these little reminders would pop up like mushrooms, and my wife and I would stop whatever we were doing, whether we were mad, or sad, or content, and we would suddenly laugh and think of those wagging tails.

It seemed to me that this incident kind of summed it all up. Our relationship was a lot like the story of the Danish cookie tin. Friendship was a little cookie that could make a bad day seem good for a few minutes. And the wrappers we kept finding years later were great reminders of how lucky I was to have had such a friend. Every wrapper I found brought a warm, happy smile to my face. Those memories helped me get through a lot of days.

||||||||||||||||||||

Exley has been gone for some time now, but he is not dead. Whenever there are large family gatherings, he is remembered with fondness and hilarity, love and warmth by many. He instantly comes back to life, wandering around the table or living room, filling the room with laughter and good cheer. He may not take up a space on the couch any longer, but he rests quietly in my heart. His lessons and love are with me and my family, every day of our lives.

A TRUE FRIEND IS A FRIEND FOR LIFE

SECRETS TO REMEMBER

- Friends can be demanding; in that way they bring out the best in us.

- Friendship is something that keeps on giving to us even when our friend is no longer there.

- Friends are the truly invaluable things we all can count among our possessions.

- Friendship requires effort, patience, humor, anger, honesty, flattery, and love.

EPILOGUE

"He lifted his head and looked at me, then put
his head in my lap, nuzzling me with his nose as
he had done the first time I had seen him as a
puppy. I told him I had to go and that I would
miss him. He looked at me again and licked my
cheek. 'Thank you, boy,' I whispered. Then I
left without looking back."
—*Willie Morris,* My Dog Skip

Exley was never much one for boundaries. Given a fenced yard,
he invariably found a way out. He might have wandered far in his
escape, but he always came home. I always did my best in these in-
stances to stop or impede his transgressions, but he was relentless.

We went to visit friends in Maine one time, and he simply
jumped the fence and ran off into the Maine woods, coming
back an hour later, covered in mud and smelling of the forest.

My mother-in-law, Evelyn Hoover, lives in France. She
comes and visits every other year. Some have been good trips
and some have been bad: a heat wave, a series of heavy snows,

fighting with her brother when they traveled together, a pleasant spring, a hot but nice summer. These things happen. But her comfort and companion when she visited was Exley. She loved the hound in him. And he was a gentle, loving soul.

Evelyn had written Dominique from France of the French Basque news and weather, discussing her plans for an upcoming visit. At the end of the letter, she wrote, " . . . and tell Exley to wait for me." But he did not. Evelyn wrote that she was very sad the day she got the news. She was not the only one. My parents, aunts, uncles, and friends were all sad—at his passing and for me.

But I think on it now, and I marvel how this dog, a simple pet, an extravagance in many parts of the world, became so important and so loved by so many. And how his passing left so big a hole in so many lives.

"Heaven goes by favor. If it went by merit, you would stay out, and your dog would go in," wrote Mark Twain. Any good dog lover knows Twain to be absolutely right on this count, and I chuckle every time I read this quote. I am a God-fearing man. But I must admit that like others, I sometimes have my doubts about an afterlife. I'm going to die someday; it will have been a heck of a run, no matter when the alarm clock sounds. After Exley's death, someone told me that I would meet my dog again in heaven. The sentiment is lovely, and would that I could, I would give a lot to see him. He has visited me in my dreams.

"If there are no dogs in heaven," Will Rogers once said, "then I want to go where they went." Heaven or no, Exley has left me with a lifetime of memories and friendship, and he did so with others as well. He left a lifetime of friends wanting more, and isn't that the best thing you can say about anyone?

And now it is time to begin anew. Two months later, we rescued a Dalmatian called Chief. He was 6 years old. He was raised from a pup by a woman who had died of an incurable disease, and the widower, an executive who traveled extensively, gave him to a rescue group to find another home.

Personally, I was not ready for a new dog. My heart had welled up like a fist, and it was closed. But Chelsea was inconsolable, and sadness was written all over her face. She needed a companion. Especially in her older age, we wanted her to have a friend to be home with during the course of the day.

I thought back to my old friend Bentley, and I knew few

children who didn't like Dalmatians. The boys were still sad at the loss of their old friend, and the addition of a Dalmatian (one of their favorite movies was *101 Dalmatians*) and the novelty of the Dalmatian, I thought, would set the household in a new direction.

Dalmatians require lots of exercise, and Dominique was worried, because our focus was now on the boys. She was worried that we would not have enough time or energy to devote to another dog. But she gritted her teeth and made contact with a number of Dalmatian rescue clubs. We found Chief, one of the laziest and handsomest animals I have ever met. If there is such a thing as reincarnation, Chief's current demeanor is certainly the result of a lifetime of grueling work and utter torment, because I do not know a more spoiled and sleepier dog.

We took two cars to find Chief, one with the boys and me, and the other with Chelsea, our German shepherd. If Chief didn't hit it off with Chelsea, he wasn't going home with us. Luckily for him, she liked him, and he was playful and affectionate. We agreed that I would take Chief in our Jetta, and my wife would ride home with the boys and Chelsea in the station wagon.

Chief was a gentle soul. He got into the backseat, tall, lean, and muscular, and lay down in the center of the seat. As I got in, Chief calmly laid his head down on the armrest between the two seats and dozed comfortably as we drove home.

I was filled with mixed emotions. This new animal was a great new opportunity. But I was filled with longing that I might turn around and see Exley instead. My eyes misted over, and I got lost, missing my exit. I drove around the highways and countrysides of Pennsylvania and New Jersey for an hour before finding my way back to the path home. But never did Chief budge from his spot. He nuzzled my elbow a couple of times and only once did he get up, lick my face, and then get back into the same exact position as he was in before.

Chief settled in very easily. He was a short-haired, speckled dog, much like Exley. Without encouragement, he took up Exley's old spots on the couch, the dog bed in our bedroom. He even lay down in the same spot Exley had chosen in the kitchen.

Chief was the right decision. He is the spoiled love child of my wife, Dominique, whom he adores with unrivaled and unrepentant favor. He is her shadow. And for his unabashed admiration, he is allowed many more privileges than any dog before him. And the boys love him. Life has assumed, in the intervening years, an enjoyable, if faster, pace, it seems. The cycles of life go on.

In my better, more optimistic moments, I agree with the sentiments by renowned writer Jon Katz, who wrote in *A Dog Year,* "Like other friends and loved ones, dogs can mark periods in one's life, boundaries between one time and another."

Every once in a while, I will take a walk around the neighborhood, and I will pass our old house: the first house we had in Freehold. And I look out over the backyard from the side of the house, and I think of the dark, warm summer nights, and I think of Exley and me playing with the light saber in the dark backyard. And I look at the stairs of the house through the window of the front door, and I can still imagine him waiting for me on the steps.

But I must continue my walk. We move on, appreciative for the friendships we have come to know and cherish and open to the new opportunities that God extends us each and every day.

ACKNOWLEDGMENTS

First, the author must acknowledge and commend Nancy Campbell, who trusted me and who introduced me to Spike in October of 1992. My debt to her can never be repaid.

She was also one of the people who introduced me to my wife, a debt which is priceless. Second, I would like to thank my many dog friends over the years, including, but not limited to, Kristina Johnsen and Haxa, Tar, and Russia, Cindy and Maureen and their puppies, Rob and Kiah, Neela Banerjee and Rohan, Tony and Daisy, Lesley Williams, Vanessa Thompson and the rest of the Park Slope dog people, Bob and Lulu, Joan Tabor, Ken and Judy Marden, Mark Campbell, Jim and Lia Prendergast, Jeanne and Eric Hirsch, Matt Weismantle, Natalka Pavlovsky, James and Diane McGuiness, and to my editorial friends and cohorts in the early years, Rick Wolff, Rob McMahon, and Ken Samelson.

Special thanks to Amy Ammen, my coauthor on my two dog books, and a wonderful person. Thanks, Amy.

Of course, there are others. I have to thank my parents, Philip and Joanne De Vito of Lawrenceville, New Jersey, and

Eugenio and Anna Maria Venanzi, of Stamford, Connecticut, and my sisters, Claudia Pazmany and Leigh Ann De Vito, and my brother, Eugene T. Venanzi II. My parents have always taught us a love of animals, especially dogs, and we share that love with each other. I thank them for their patience with me and with Exley over the years.

Any author of such an effort also owes a huge debt of gratitude to those who went before him. Several writers' works have proved invaluable to me. Willie Morris's incredible tale *My Dog Skip,* Elizabeth Marshall Thomas's *The Hidden Life of Dogs,* and Caroline Knapp's *Pack of Two* were indispensable. The writings of behaviorist Ian Dunbar were always near, as were Clarence Pfaffenberger's *The New Knowledge of Dog Behavior* and Paul Loeb's and Suzanne Hlavacek's *Smarter Than You Think.* Other invaluable works that I consulted during the writing of this book included Jeffrey Moussaieff Masson's *Dogs Never Lie about Love,* Jon Katz's two great works *A Dog Year* and *The New Work of Dogs,* Jan Fennell's *The Dog Listener,* Trish King's innovative *Parenting Your Dog,* Susan Chernak McElroy's *Animals as Guides for the Soul,* and the works of Stanley Coren and Roger A. Caras.

I would also like to thank Susan Petersen Kennedy, president of Penguin Group USA for her acquiescence in allowing me to pursue this project, despite my obligations and responsibilities to her and my staff on Hudson Street. Without her cheerful assent, this opportunity would have passed beyond my reach.

As ever, I owe a debt of special thanks in all my professional endeavors to Gilbert King for his ear, opinions, advice, general good cheer, and encouragement.

Special thanks to www.fidobrooklyn.org for their help and encouragement.

I would, of course, like to thank my editor, Zach Schisgal, who helped make this book a reality. Were it not for his excitement and enthusiasm, I might have at any time given up under the massive weight of such an undertaking. He was cheerleader, coach, and friend. I thank him for his tireless editing and opinions. He was truly the best editor a writer could ever hope to have. I thank him for this opportunity as well as all those at Rodale Books. I would also like to thank Courtney Conroy for all her help and efforts as well.

I would like to thank my agent and friend, Gene Brissie, for his urging me to put this story down in pen and ink, and Edward Claflin of James Peter Associates. I thank them for their encouragement and assistance and their belief in me.

I would like to thank my two sons, whose patience has been stretched between my day job and the call of our barn, wherein the writing of this work took place. I have sacrificed weeks of hours working in the barn and owe them a great debt of time well spent with them in more important pursuits in their eyes—swordplay, T-ball, the making of paper airplanes, riding bicycles, and many other pastimes. I thank them for letting me do this, and I pledge to become more competent at Game Boy, GameCube, and PlayStation.

And finally, I would like to thank my wife, Dominique. She is the real animal lover in our household and a premiere animal book publisher. Dominique is the real guardian of our family's pets. She makes the vet appointments, keeps us up on all the latest dog training, behavior, nutrition, and health news. She is the groomer, nurse, chef, homeopathic pharmacist, and mommy of our dog den. She was my friend, counselor, confessor, secretary, expert, confidante, and pillar during the writing of this book. Would that she could, I am sure she would trade any of my books for some more time spent with me and our kids. My successes in my job and work are a result of her effort, love, and understanding. She makes my failures and disappointments seem inconsequential. I thank her most of all.